First World War
and Army of Occupation
War Diary
France, Belgium and Germany

34 DIVISION
103 Infantry Brigade
Princess Louise's (Argyll & Sutherland Highlanders)
1/5th Battalion
and King's Own Scottish Borderers 5th Battalion
1 April 1918 - 31 March 1919

WO95/2466/1

The Naval & Military Press Ltd
www.nmarchive.com
Published in association with The National Archives

Published by

The Naval & Military Press Ltd

Unit 10 Ridgewood Industrial Park,
Uckfield, East Sussex,
TN22 5QE England
Tel: +44 (0) 1825 749494

www.naval-military-press.com

www.nmarchive.com

This diary has been reprinted in facsimile from the original. Any imperfections are inevitably reproduced and the quality may fall short of modern type and cartographic standards.

© **Crown Copyright**
Images reproduced by permission of The National Archives, London, England, 2015.

Contents

Document type	Place/Title	Date From	Date To
Heading	WO95/2466/1 5 Bn Argyle & Sutherland Highlanders 1918 April-1919 March.		
Heading	34th Division 103rd Infy Bde 1-5th Bn A. & S. Hdrs 1918 Apl-1919 Mar From Egy Pt 52 Div 157 Bde.		
Heading	52nd Division 157th Infy Bde 34 Div 103 Bde 1-5th Bn A. & S. Hdrs Apr-Jun 1918.		
Heading	157th Brigade 52nd Division. Disembarked Marseilles From Egypt 17.4.18 1/5th Battalion Argyle & Sutherland Highlanders April 1918.		
War Diary		01/04/1918	11/04/1918
War Diary	Kaiser I Hind	11/04/1918	17/04/1918
War Diary	Marseilles	18/04/1918	20/04/1918
War Diary	Train.	21/04/1918	30/04/1918
Heading	War Diary 1/5th A & S.H. 1st-31st May 1918 Vol 2.		
War Diary	Aire.	01/05/1918	06/05/1918
War Diary	M.S. Eloi.	06/05/1918	31/05/1918
Map	Disposition.		
War Diary	In The Field.	01/06/1918	30/06/1918
Miscellaneous	Raid Orders by Lieut Col. C.L. Barlow D.S.O. Commdg 5th Battn A & S Highrs.		
Miscellaneous	Nominal Roll Of Officers 1/5th A. & S.H. At 28/ June 1918.	28/06/1918	28/06/1918
Miscellaneous	List Of Casualties During June 1918.		
War Diary	St. Janter Biezen.	01/07/1918	07/07/1918
War Diary	W. Of Bengneux	29/07/1918	31/07/1918
War Diary	In The Field.	01/08/1918	30/09/1918
War Diary	Zero House.	01/10/1918	01/10/1918
War Diary	Zandvoorde.	02/10/1918	02/10/1918
War Diary	Wervicq.	03/10/1918	05/10/1918
War Diary	Kruickseek.	06/10/1918	12/10/1918
War Diary	Kruickseek Area.	13/10/1918	14/10/1918
War Diary	Menin.	15/10/1918	16/10/1918
War Diary	Menin Area.	17/10/1918	19/10/1918
War Diary	Knock Area.	20/10/1918	26/10/1918
War Diary	St. Anne Area.	27/10/1918	27/10/1918
War Diary	Hulote.	28/10/1918	28/10/1918
War Diary	Keijtbery.	29/10/1918	31/10/1918
War Diary	Boschkant.	01/11/1918	01/11/1918
War Diary	Sterhoek.	02/11/1918	03/11/1918
War Diary	Bisseghem.	04/11/1918	08/11/1918
War Diary	Halluin.	09/11/1918	16/11/1918
War Diary	St. Sauveur.	17/11/1918	18/11/1918
War Diary	Wannebecq.	19/11/1918	12/12/1918
War Diary	Graty.	13/12/1918	19/12/1918
War Diary	Wepion.	20/12/1918	23/12/1918
War Diary	Auvelais.	24/12/1918	20/01/1919
War Diary	En Route	20/01/1919	21/01/1919
War Diary	Geistingen.	21/01/1919	01/02/1919
War Diary	Geistingen Siegburg.	02/02/1919	02/02/1919
War Diary	Siegburg Wahn.	03/02/1919	03/02/1919

War Diary	Wahn.	04/02/1919	23/02/1919
War Diary	Wahn Hennef.	24/02/1919	24/02/1919
War Diary	Hennef.	25/02/1919	28/02/1919
Heading	War Diary Of 1/5th Argyll & Sutherland Highlanders. 1st March 1919 to 31st March 1919. Volume 6.		
War Diary	Hennef.	01/03/1919	07/03/1919
War Diary	Wahn.	08/03/1919	08/03/1919
War Diary	Enzen.	09/03/1919	11/03/1919
War Diary	Bergerhausen.	12/03/1919	31/03/1919
Miscellaneous	III Namur1/100,000. AISH.		
Map	Namur.		
Miscellaneous	III Namur 1/100,000. AISH.		
Map	Tournai.		
Map	For Official Use On.		
Miscellaneous	I Tournai 5 1/100,000 Aish.		
Miscellaneous	2/Lieuts		
Diagram etc	Brussels 6. Edition 2. Belgium.		
Map	Belgium 1:100,000.		
Diagram etc	Brussels 6. Edition 2. Belgium Scale 1/100,000.		
Heading	WO95/2466/2 5 Bn King's Own Scottish Borderers 1918 April-1919 March.		
Heading	155th Brigade 52nd Division Battalion disembarked Marseilles From Egypt 17.4.18. 1/5th Battalion King's Own Scottish Borderers April 1918.		
Miscellaneous	3rd Section B.E.T.	04/05/1917	04/05/1917
War Diary	Sarona.	01/04/1918	01/04/1918
War Diary	Surafend Near Ludd.	02/04/1918	04/04/1918
War Diary	Kantara.	05/04/1918	05/04/1918
War Diary	Alexandria.	06/04/1918	14/04/1918
War Diary	Hmt Kaiser-I-Hind.	15/04/1918	16/04/1918
War Diary	Marseilles.	17/04/1918	17/04/1918
War Diary	Mosso Camp.	17/04/1918	18/04/1918
War Diary	Train.	19/04/1918	21/04/1918
War Diary	Forest Montiers.	22/04/1918	28/04/1918
War Diary	Witte.	29/04/1918	30/04/1918
Miscellaneous	1/5th K.O.S. Borders.		
Heading	52nd Division 155th Infy Bde 34 Div 103 Bde 1-5th Bn K.O.S.B. Apr-Jun 1918.		
Heading	War Diary Of 1/5th Kings Own Scottish Borderers 1-5-18-31-5-18 Vol XXXVII.		
War Diary	Witte.	01/05/1918	06/05/1918
War Diary	Neuville St Vaast.	07/05/1918	12/05/1918
War Diary	St Eloy.	13/05/1918	19/05/1918
War Diary	Mont St Eloy.	20/05/1918	23/05/1918
War Diary	Vimy T.25.A.5.8.	24/05/1918	27/05/1918
War Diary	Vimy T.20.c.2.1.	28/05/1918	31/05/1918
Miscellaneous	1/5 Ko & Boedeue.		
Heading	War Diary Of 1/5 1/2nd King's Own Scottish Borderers 1-6-1918-30-6-1918 Vol XXXVIII.		
War Diary	Vimy T.16.c.9.3.	01/06/1918	04/06/1918
War Diary	Vimy.	05/06/1918	11/06/1918
War Diary	Mont St Eloy.	12/06/1918	19/06/1918
War Diary	Thelus Caves.	20/05/1918	22/05/1918
War Diary	Thelus Caves A.6.c.6.7.	22/06/1918	27/06/1918
War Diary	Oost Capel.	28/06/1918	29/06/1918
War Diary	St Janster Biezen.	30/06/1918	30/06/1918

Miscellaneous	To: Lieut-Colonel R.N. Coulson, the Officers, Warrant Officers, Non-Commissioned Officers and Men Of The King's Own Scottish Borderers. Vol XXXVIII Appendix 2.	26/06/1918	26/06/1918
Miscellaneous	Dear Colonel Coulson. Vol XXXVIII Appendix 3.	27/06/1918	27/06/1918
Miscellaneous	Vol XXXVIII Appendix 4.		
Miscellaneous	1/5 K.O. & Border Of Appendix No 1. To War Diary For Month Of June 1918.		
Heading	34th Division 103rd Infy Bde 1-5th K.O.S. Bdrs. 1918 Apl-1919 Mar From Egypt 52 Div 155 Bde To Lowland Bde 9 Div.		
Heading	War Diary Of 1/5th King's Own Scottish Borderers From 1.7.1918 To 31.7.1918 Vol XXXIX.		
War Diary	St Janster Biezen.	01/07/1918	07/07/1918
War Diary	Cormette Q.35.d.3.4.	07/07/1918	13/07/1918
War Diary	Proven F.1.d.2.5 Sheet 27.	13/07/1918	17/07/1918
War Diary	Chamant.	18/07/1918	19/07/1918
War Diary	Feigneux (Beauvais L.3.2.2).	19/07/1918	19/07/1918
War Diary	Feigneux.	20/07/1918	20/07/1918
War Diary	Soucy.	20/07/1918	22/07/1918
War Diary	Montram Boeuf.	23/07/1918	26/07/1918
War Diary	Bois De Boeuf.	27/07/1918	28/07/1918
War Diary	Bois De Baillette.	28/07/1918	31/07/1918
War Diary	Beugneux.	31/07/1918	31/07/1918
War Diary	Bois De Baillette.		
Miscellaneous	34th Division Instructions No.1. General Scheme. Appendix No.1. Vol XXXIX.		
Operation(al) Order(s)	103rd Infantry Brigade Order No 225. Appendix No.2. Vol XXXIX.	28/07/1918	28/07/1918
Miscellaneous	Brigade Wire B.M. 176 5th Bn. K.O.S.B. Appendix S. Vol XXXIX.	29/07/1918	29/07/1918
Operation(al) Order(s)	103rd Infantry Brigade Order No. 226. Appendix IV. Vol XXXIX.	31/07/1918	31/07/1918
Heading	War-Diary Of 1/5th King's Own Scottish Borderers From 1-8-18-31-8-18 Vol XL.		
War Diary	Beugneux.	01/08/1918	03/08/1918
War Diary	Dammartin.	04/08/1918	06/08/1918
War Diary	Wormhoot.	07/08/1918	14/08/1918
War Diary	Jan Ter Beizen Ary.	15/08/1918	15/08/1918
War Diary	Dirty Bucket Area.	16/08/1918	21/08/1918
War Diary	Ypres.	21/08/1918	21/08/1918
War Diary	Left Sector.	24/08/1918	26/08/1918
War Diary	Ypres.	26/08/1918	30/08/1918
War Diary	Zevecotin.	31/08/1918	31/08/1918
Miscellaneous	1/5th King's Own Scottish Borderers.		
Miscellaneous	1/5th King's Own Scottish Border.	09/08/1918	09/08/1918
Miscellaneous	1/5 K.O.S.B Casualty Return. Appendix 6.	09/08/1918	09/08/1918
Miscellaneous	Appendix No 10 War Diary For July 1918. Appendix 9.		
Miscellaneous	1/5 King's Own Scottish Borderers. Appendix 7.	09/08/1918	09/08/1918
Diagram etc	Positions Of Assembles & Deployment. Appendix I.		
Miscellaneous	H.Q. 103 Inf Bde.	07/10/1918	07/10/1918
Heading	War Diary Of 1/5th King's Own Scottish Borderers From 1-9-18 To 30-9-18 Vol XLI.		
War Diary	Kemmel.	01/09/1918	01/09/1918
War Diary	Kemmel (Lindenhook) Rd.	01/09/1918	02/09/1918
War Diary	Scherpenberg.	03/09/1918	03/09/1918

War Diary	Kemmel.	04/09/1918	08/09/1918
War Diary	St Eloi	09/09/1918	09/09/1918
War Diary	Steenvoorde.	10/09/1918	10/09/1918
War Diary	Hellebroucq.	11/09/1918	20/09/1918
War Diary	Wytschaete.	21/09/1918	30/09/1918
Operation(al) Order(s)	1/5th K.O.S.B. Operation Order No. 10. Vol XVI Operation Order I.		
Miscellaneous			
Miscellaneous	1/5 King's Own Scottish Borderers Casualty List.		
Miscellaneous	1/5 Bn King's Own Scottish Borderers. Vol XLI Appendix III.		
Miscellaneous	Addendum to Lamb		
Operation(al) Order(s)	Addendum To Bn Order No. 10.		
Miscellaneous			
Miscellaneous	Administrative Orders.		
Miscellaneous			
Heading	War Diary Of 1/5th Kings Own Scottish Borderers From 1/10/18 To 31/10/18 Vol XLII.		
War Diary	Zamvoorde	01/10/1918	02/10/1918
War Diary	Wervicq.	03/10/1918	31/10/1918
Miscellaneous	War Diary, 6 October, 1918 Appendix I. Congratulatory Messages To The Battalion.		
Miscellaneous	Appendix No 1. to War Diary, October 1918.		
Miscellaneous	1/5th King's Own Scottish Borderers.		
Miscellaneous	1/5 King's Own Scottish Borderers.		
Heading	War Diary Of 1/5th King's Own Scottish Borderers T.F. From 1/11/18 To 30/11/18 Volume XLIII.		
War Diary	Ref. Map Sheet 29 N.E. 1/20,000.	01/11/1918	02/11/1918
War Diary	Ref. Map Sheet 29 N.W. 1/20,000.	03/11/1918	14/11/1918
War Diary	Ref Map. Tournai. 5.	14/11/1918	17/11/1918
War Diary	Ogy.	18/11/1918	30/11/1918
Operation(al) Order(s)	1/5 King's Own Scottish Borderers Operation Order No. 22.	02/11/1918	02/11/1918
Miscellaneous	1/5 K.O.S. Borderers.	02/11/1918	02/11/1918
Miscellaneous	1/5 K.O.S. Borderers After Order by Lieutenant Colonel F.G. Comtenay Hood D.S.O. Commdg.	05/11/1918	05/11/1918
Operation(al) Order(s)	Battalion King's Own Scottish Borderers. Operation Order No. 24.	13/11/1918	13/11/1918
Miscellaneous	Battalion King's Own Scottish Borderers Operation Order No.	14/11/1918	14/11/1918
Miscellaneous	0.4.00 To C.O Leeze.	01/11/1918	01/11/1918
Miscellaneous	C.C. Leeze.		
Operation(al) Order(s)	Battalion Kings Own Scottish Borderers. Operation Order No. 27.	15/11/1918	15/11/1918
Operation(al) Order(s)	Battalion K.O.S.B Operation Order No. 28.	11/11/1918	11/11/1918
Heading	War Diary Of 1/5th Kings Own Scottish Borderers From 1/12/18 To 31/12/18 Volume XLIV.		
War Diary		01/12/1918	31/12/1918
Miscellaneous	1/5th. Battalion King's Own Scottish Borderers.	09/01/1919	09/01/1919
Heading	War Diary Of 1/5th King's Own Scottish Borderers From 1/1/19 To 31/1/19 Volume XLV.		
War Diary		01/01/1919	12/01/1919
War Diary	Auvelais.	13/01/1919	22/01/1919
War Diary	Menden.	23/01/1919	31/01/1919
Heading	War Diary Of 1/5th Bn King's Own Scottish Borderers From 1/2/19 To 28/2/19 Volume XLVI.		

War Diary	Menden.	01/02/1919	02/02/1919
War Diary	Wahn.	03/02/1919	23/02/1919
War Diary	Seelscheid.	23/02/1919	28/02/1919
Heading	War Diary Of 1/5th Bn King's Own Scottish Borderers From 1/3/19 To 31/3/19 Vol XLVII.		
War Diary	Wahn.	01/03/1919	01/03/1919
War Diary	Solingen.	02/03/1919	31/03/1919
Miscellaneous	1/5th. Battalion King's Own Scottish Borderers.	08/03/1919	08/03/1919
Miscellaneous	Captain July Dickie for War Diary.		

WO 95 2466/1

5 BN ARGYLE & SUTHERLAND
HIGHLANDERS
1918 APRIL – 1919 MARCH

34TH DIVISION
103RD INFY BDE

1-5TH BN A. & S. HDRS

~~JLY — DEC 1918~~

1918 APL — 1919 MAR

FROM EGYPT 52 DIV 157 BDE

ATTACHED

52ND DIVISION
157TH INFY BDE

34 DIV
103 BDE

1-5TH BN A. & S. HDRS
APR - JUN 1918

157th Brigade.

52nd Division.

Disembarked MARSEILLES from EGYPT 17.4.18.

1/5th BATTALION

ARGYLE & SUTHERLAND HIGHLANDERS

APRIL 1918.

WAR DIARY or INTELLIGENCE SUMMARY

Army Form C. 2118

5 Qy S/H Volume 2

S.M.

Place	Date 1918	Hour	Summary of Events and Information	Remarks and references to Appendices
	April 1st		Lt. Cunningham & 2/Lt R. proceed to Sarona today as advance party for Batt. Battalion being relieved by Rot. Punjabis on night 2/3rd. Preliminary instructions to Coys. 1/55 & 1/56 Brigades there to Ludd today. Turks shell our line heavy shells. No casualties.	
	2nd "		Prepare for move. Advance party of relieving Battalion (20 Punjabis) arrive in camp 2050. Battalion relieved 2150 and proceed to Sarona. Arrive Sarona 2400 and stay in bivies overnight.	
	3rd "		Battalion march to Surafend Camp (2 Kilo. W. of Ludd) Strength 38 Officers 974 ORs.	
	4th "		At Surafend. All special articles received on E.E.F. Mobile Scale returned to D.A.D.O.S. C.O. and St. Grant proceed on short leave to Egypt.	
	5th "		At Surafend.	
	6th "		Leave Camp 1450 and entrain at Ludd. Move off at 1751. Entraining State 38 Offrs. 966 ORs.	
	7th "		Arrive Kantara E. 1030. Bivouac at No. 2 I.B.D. Leave bivouac area 2315. Entrain and move off 0150. Drafts of 9 offrs. 666 ORs. join. Enbarking Strength.	
	8th "		R.Coy. 19 offrs. 288 OR; B.coy. 6 offr 253 OR, C.coy. 6 offr. 254 OR; D.coy. 9 offr. 241 ORs. Arrive Gabbary Quay, Alexandria 1045, and entrain direct on H.M.T. Kaiser-i-Hind No. 2. Embarkation complete 1500. Nominal Roll of personnel entraining attached:- Offrs 44; WOs 7; Sgts 51; Cpls & L/Cpls 23; privates 894. C.O. rejoins. Shore leave officers & WOs only.	
	9th "		Kaiser-i-Hind. Lt. Col. Morrison rejoins from G.H.Q. Cairo.	
	10th "	1600	Ship draws out to moorings in Harbour. — Coys. short route march through Alexandria during forenoon.	
	11th "	1430	Leave Harbour.	
		1700	Arrive at Rendez-vous and convoy formed.	

WAR DIARY or INTELLIGENCE SUMMARY

Army Form C. 2118

Vol. 2.

Place	Date 1918	Hour	Summary of Events and Information	Remarks and references to Appendices
Tarar. S. Third	April 11th		Tarar. S. Third Canberra } Australian Malwa Indara } ships Caledonia Orvieto Leoti Castle Frank 8 Destroyers	
do	12th		Seaplane escorts convoy till darkness set it.	
do	13th		Ships Routine. O.C. inspection of ship. 1030 derby. All ranks at Boat Station. Rifles placed in ships Armory. Weather good. Wind N.W. Slight Swell. Convoy Formation :- [diagram] Ships Routine.	
do	14th		Time put back 1 hour. i.e. to Greenwich Summer Time. Wind fresh from N. Beam Sea. Confined Prev. Conf. E. Revise.	
do	15th		Ships Routine. Weather Cold and good sea running.	
do	16th		— do — Duty Battalion.	
do	17th	0830	Arrive Marseilles. 2nd ship to enter harbour. Aeroplane, Observation Balloon and torpedo craft meet convoy. Misty weather.	
		1400	Disembark March off to No.10 Rest Camp (Pinon Camp) reached 1630. (Baggage brought by M.T.) Good camping area. Rations good. Order of march D.C.B.A. Rations late.	
Marseilles	18th		hot morning. Rations late.	
do	19th		Preparation made for departure.	
do	20th	0120	March to Marseilles Station. Entrain at Arenc Plat 1. 41 Offrs 1020 O.Rs. 11 Absentees. Order of March C.A.B.D.	

Army Form C. 2118

Vol. 2

WAR DIARY
or
INTELLIGENCE SUMMARY
(Erase heading not required.)

Instructions regarding War Diaries and Intelligence Summaries are contained in F.S. Regs., Part II. and the Staff Manual respectively. Title Pages will be prepared in manuscript.

Place	Date 1918	Hour	Summary of Events and Information	Remarks and references to Appendices
Manoeuvre	April 20	0553	Leave Station.	
Train	-	1810	El Teil. Leave 1950. Tea issued.	
"	21st	0920	Arrive Paron le Monial. Leave 1040. Tea issued. Men wash. Battery exd.	
"	"	1250	Pass through Noviellons	
"	22	1240	Gournay	
		1800	arrive	
		2040	Arrive. Arrive Noyelles Platoon 10.15 pm. Tramp 600 yds from Station Camp, How Pende. Arrive 1110. B+D Lanchino. A. Talleville. (Month of Somme Area).	
	23rd	0810	Batt move off to Billeting area. - Coy. How Pende. Arrive 1110. B+D Lanchino. A. Talleville. (Month of Somme Area).	
			Transport drawn from Abbeville. Horses, mules, wagons, rations, kits etc.	
	24th		Biscuits	
	25th		Gen. Still visits area. All surplus kit sent to Bee Hallow from Tomorrow home.	
	26th			
	27th		Lt Dunn + O.R. proceed with Bn party to new area.	
	28th		Bn Order to move received 10.10 pm. Battalion rendezvous Cross Roads 1000 yds S.W. of S. Valence.	
R. Sigs. 29th 3/5/18	29th		Battalion present at rendezvous 0300. Move off Kentain A B+C Cos at Noyelles 0730. Arrive Bergnette 1515 and march to Cavalry Barracks. Aire. Arrive 1740. D Coy arrive 2030.	
	30th		Officers on reconnaissance to secure defence line.	

E L Barlow Lieut. Col.
Comdg. 5th Bn A.&S. Hidors

1875 Wt. W5193;826 1,000,000 4/15 J.B.C. & A. A.D.S.S./Forms/C. 2118.

WAR DIARY
1/5th A & S.H.
1st – 31st May, 1918.

Army Form C. 2118

WAR DIARY
or
INTELLIGENCE SUMMARY
(Erase heading not required.)

May 1918   Vol. III Sheet 1

Place	Date	Hour	Summary of Events and Information	Remarks and references to Appendices
AIRE	MAY 1st		Batt. prepared to proceed. Fatigue parties ordered. Capt. Taylor appointed Adjt. vice Lt. Grant. Officers reconnoitre reserve line thro' XI Corps	
	2nd		Batt. made march to RENE where Batt. completes underground gas mask test.	
	3rd		Training within. Officers instructed beginners in Lewis Gun Staff on recent operations. Lectures — C.R.E. & G.R.A. XI Corps Staff. I. Morrison C. in C. visits Lecture Room and in a short address welcomes Reichen Officers.	
	4th		Musketry. Lewis Gun fire on 30 yds range. Lt. Barr & 6 O.R. Advance Party proceed to Bruay Lourde.	
	5th		Batt. transport proceed to new area by road.	
M. St. ELOI	6th		Batt. entrained at AIRE 0305 (38 Offrs + 854 O.R.) Arrived MAROEUIL 1530 and march to M. St. Eloi where Batt. is accommodated in huts etc.	
	7th		C.O. & O.C. Coys proceed in advance to LA CHAUDIERE AREA (VIMY) & await arrival of Batt. Batt. relieves 102nd Pennsylvania in LA CHAUDIERE area — front line — (A Coy in disposition near) Brimstone (3 Offrs) B & C Coys centre. B Coy L. and D Coy in reserve. Branch routine. Enemy expected to attack. Leave to U.K. open for Division.	
	8th		Military arrangements of ... the approach not so good as in E.E.F. Disposition altered. Branch routine. Capt. J. Morrison to Div. of Gen. as Staines Officer.	
	9th		Held in supports only (as sketch). Lt. S.R. Thompson on U.K. Leave — Birmingham	
	10th		Batt. in command of Lt. Col. Obij.	
			Misty morning. Front line ... eighty. Lt. Grant proceeds to Corps Lewis Gun Course. Capt. P. Rucker to command of A Coy. (temp.)	
	11th		Quiet within. Our patrols had difficulty in getting through our own wire.	

WAR DIARY
or
INTELLIGENCE SUMMARY
(Erase heading not required.)

Army Form C. 2118.

Vol III Sheet 11

Place	Date	Hour	Summary of Events and Information	Remarks and references to Appendices
	12th		...visits Major Curtis GSO2 met the line. Quiet day.	
	13		Relieved by 6th H.L.I. ...330 ... go back as the supporting Batt. Lieut Crosby Brown LINE taken over HQ 5th H.L.I. Patrol Party. Whole Bn arr in original depth. Lieut E U.K. sick D.	
	14		Training & Defence Recce	
	15		Normal routine Work on Defence lines continued	
	16		do	
	17		L.O. Transferred to U.K. on leave. Lt DPMcDonald → Capt Van Schuyl. Coy in graveside:—	
			Trench Strength 1 N.C.O. & O.R.	
			Platoon 1 Off. - 31 "	
			" " " - 31 "	
			" " 6 " - 42 "	
			O.C. H.Q. 6 - 77 "	
			Act surplus personnel to abnce formed to obtain camp when Maj Ogburn	
			Orderly; French Recces work continued	
	19		Relieve 6th H.L.I. in front line trenches B Coy — TEDDIE GERARD DCoy TEDDIE GERARD-KENE	
			A Coy on left ACTRESS BETTY GLADYS C Coy on right HESTOR DORIS B Coy relieved by 11 pm	
	20		Coy Cmdr Lt Gen made trench line & inspected B Coy	
	21st		Capt — O.M. W. J. Watson on U.K. leave	
	22nd		French recces	
	23		do 11pm supporting bn for Germ trench raid carried out at 02.45	

WAR DIARY
or
INTELLIGENCE SUMMARY

Army Form C. 2118.
Vol III Sheet III

Place	Date	Hour	Summary of Events and Information	Remarks and references to Appendices
	May 23rd		(Contd.) on at prosency hurreled from Billy BURNE TRENCH (1700 effective men). Wind strong but favourable. NB gas alarm heard from enemy's lines. Our casualties nil. Smith	
	24th		System reported close of gas O330. Relieved by 4th R.S. (Col. Richardson) (c/o march casualties. Winter rd + work). Relief complete by 10 p.m. arrive in new camp NEUVILLE-ST-VAAST 11 p.m. (Estimated) Div. Reserve	
	25th		As independently. Rest	
	26th		Learned to washing, drying and inspection. Lewis Service. Y.M.C.A. Lt. Q.R. Roman rejoins from leave.	
	27th		Company Commanders as per attached syllabus	
	28th		Batt. on fatigue hunting cable 1000-1045. camp chelsea	
	29th		Training contd. Lt. Graham & M.K. Evans	
	30th		Training contd. R.G.S.	
	31st		Training contd. (O.C. specs A Coy + Batt. report inspects C Coy at tactical scheme 10 a.m. HQ.) spades practise Grenade. engineers. Officers Nets in arriving respect. Chasseurd under Capt Hargreaves + B+H. training cards. Capt. Rive att'd + Start Range 2 Km east. 5 minutes 7.30	
			Stacey fit Applesham 15 August	

	Effective attached	Detached	Fighting Strength	
	O	OR	O	OR	O	OR
	40	1025	12	186	28	839

Lieut. Col.
Comdg. 5th. Bn. A. & S. Highrs

WAR DIARY
or
INTELLIGENCE SUMMARY

Army Form C. 2118.

5 A98 H

Vol. IV. Sheet I

Place	Date	Hour	Summary of Events and Information	Remarks and references to Appendices
In the Field	June 1916 1st		Battalion in Hanson Camp. Coy Training continued as usual. 5 Officers & 40 OR. attend Demonstration on Nature of Mustard Gas. Battalion prepares to relieve 8th Scottish Rifles.	
	2nd		Divine Service as usual. C.O. inspects Camp at 1030. C.O. to Detail Camp. Major Agnew takes over Command. Card D'Coy and 1 platoon A Coy. take over W.Z. and 1 Platoon X Coy. of 8th S.R. in R.Section of 52nd Div Sector. C Coy in CANADA Trench. D Coy in BROWN line. A Coy less 1 platoon B Coy & HQ. remain in HANSON Camp	
	3rd		Parade under Coy arrangements. G.O.C. Division visits 'C' Coy area. 2/Lieut Hamilton rejoins from leave in U.K. Selected area of Enemy trench shelled - intense - 5 min. - Rapid - 5 min. Zero 1720	
	4th		Coy Parades at disposal of O.C. Coy. Lieut S.R. Morrison appointed Educational Officer for 52nd Division. - Quiet day - Enemy increased as yesterday at 1100.	
	5th		Training as usual. Lieut Talbot rejoins from School of Instruction: Enemy shell neighbourhood of Camp. Zero hour for Artillery Harassing march 1530	
	6th		Point Martin & Handley to Platoon Commanders Course XVIII Corps Inf School - Therein Parades as usual. C.O. & Adjt. visit 6th H.L.I. we relieve	
	7th		Capt. R.R. Bheaven present at 4 p.C.M. today at Wambok. Orders for Relief tomorrow received at 09.00. C.O. rejoins Unit. Major Agnew to Detail Camp Battalion takes over WILLERVAL L. Sub. Section from 6th H.L.I. Frontage 1000 yards Square Assce held. Disposition A Coy - Right; B Coy - Centre, D Coy - left; - C Coy Redorit. Coy Strength 141 oR. 2/Lieut Grant rejoins from Course. Bde Right of Division 101 Washendon / today - 155 Bde. 152% - 156 Bde 3/81% - 157 Bde 3.54 %	
	8th		1 OR. Killed, 1 OR Wounded in A Coy today by enemy shell. Front line. Line reorganised in depth - New positions occupied C.R.E and Major Curtis visit Line. Coys employed in Wiring front.	
	9th		Quiet day. Raid Orders proposed - see attached	
	10th		Lt Pages & 2 OR. & XVIII Corps Lewis Gun School. Delightful weather. Our Artillery bombard selected area in Enemy lines. Usual Patrolling	
	11th		Capt Brown rejoins from leave. - Lieut Lindsay joins Unit today. Quiet day: Col Anderson + Bde Major visit Line	
	12th		Usual Trench Routine - At night our Artillery bombard intensely for 5 min every 2 hours	
	13th		Lt Austin rejoins from leave - Quiet day Capt Gibb to UK on leave - Raid on Enemy Post - 1st Fence cut only. Raiding Party return 02.00. 14 inst. by C. Coy. Lt. G.R.Thomson i/c.	

WAR DIARY
or
INTELLIGENCE SUMMARY

(Erase heading not required.)

Army Form C. 2118.

Vol. N. Sheet II

Instructions regarding War Diaries and Intelligence Summaries are contained in F.S. Regs., Part II. and the Staff Manual respectively. Title pages will be prepared in manuscript.

Place	Date	Hour	Summary of Events and Information	Remarks and references to Appendices
In the Field	June 14th		6th H.L.I. relieve Battalion in front line – Coys take over duties from Reserve Coys of 6th H.L.I. Bn. H.Q. at Thelus Post. Pts Carmichael attends F.G.C.M. in Case of Pte Walker B Coy – as Witness	
	15th		Bn Carmichael to Hospital today — Quiet day	
	16th		C.O. & Detail Camp Major Agnew takes over command. Lieut Ringland proceeds to Sig School – Fressin. Pr. Saunders to XVIII Corps Gas School – Yressin. Capt King and 2/Lieut Goodwin rejoin Unit from leave in U.K. Divine Services as usual	
	17th		Lieut Taylor from School. Enemy shell Vimy Ridge	
	18th		2 O.R. Killed and 10 O.R. wounded today by shell fire. 2 Platoons D Coy take over THELUS Post. C Coy in HANSON Camp Pte McLeod rejoins from School Major Ramsay 4th KOSB assumed position in relief	
	19th		2/Lt Kennedy proceeds to Mushroom School Nottingham. G.O.C. inspects Throughput of Division – /5 A&SH is best turn-out. Very cold weather Capt. Robertson and 29 O.R. to Hosp. – Fever. Lieut Teller commands "A" Coy	
	20th		Battalion relieved by 4th KOSB today and proceeds by Motor to Bde Reserve Area, arrive about 17.00. HQ + 2 Coys take over LE PENDU Camp and 2 Coys Sukinshine Camp. Capt Brown, Capt Campbell + Lieut Teller to Hospital. Lieut Hunnybun assumed command of A Coy today	
	21st		2/Lieut Lindsay to Hosp. Battn attends War Prêts 6.01 backs today. Strength of Battn in Camp 24 Officers – 760 O.R. Major Agnew attends F.G.C.M. as President at Fort George. Lieut McDonald attends meeting at 13th Bde H.Q. in view of Bde Sports. The C.O. Capt King, Lt Hunnybun, Lt Hamilton & Lt Fleming attend Tank demonstration at WAVRANS	
	22nd		201319 Cpl McArthur A Coy to UK for Commission. Battalion on Brigade duties	
	23rd		Divine Services as usual – C.O. inspects Billets after Church Parade. Capt Campbell from Hosp. – Capt. Campbell to UK on leave Brigade Commander's Conference at Bde. H.Q. re. Ranges etc. Lieut Tellis was duties of Adjutant	
	24th		A Coy inspected by C.O. today – A.B. & C Coys on Gas Test. D Coy training under Coy. arrangements. All ranks attend to Recreational Training Lewis Gunners on Range	
	25th		Bn. on Bde. Duties – D Coy inspected by C.O. today Capt Brown and Pt Teller rejoin from Hosp. 2/Lt Robertson 5th Seaforths joins Unit for duty. News of going to 30th Division	
	26th		A & B. Coys on LA MOTTE Range – C Coy inspected by C.O. D Coy on FARM Course for bayonet fighting and Coy Training – Specialist under Specialist Officers. Capt Watson to Hosp today Capt King proceeds to Q. Branch 52nd Div. for duty. General Hanta – Weston inspects Battalion. 2 or 3 hundred at 1st Army HQ. for Demonstration	

WAR DIARY
INTELLIGENCE SUMMARY

Army Form C. 2118.

Vol. IV - Sheet III

Place	Date June	Hour	Summary of Events and Information	Remarks and references to Appendices
In the Field	27th		Extra Reg. men return to Battalion. 0900-1200 Reorganization of Coys. Brigade Sports at LANCASTER Camp today. Battn. 2nd in Guard Mounting and won Bombing. G.O.C. Division visits Battalion to say "Goodbye". 5,000 Frs drawn from FC	
	28th		Battalion with 5th K.O.S.B. & 8th S.R. move today for transfer from 52nd Division to 34th Division. Bn moves off in Busses at 1020, arriving at destination about midnight after 4 miles march. Route - AIRE - ST OMER - BARBEQUE. H.Q and 2 Coys at LE PENDU Camp move to Sukruba Camp. Battalion forms Advance Party - Lieut Telfer + 20 OR left in 3 motors at 0700 Battn Transport - 4 G.S. Waggons & 4 Cyclists leave at 0800 — Lieut. G.R. Thomson to First Army Inf School - HARDELOT - 4 days march.	
			STRENGTH OF UNIT	DETACHED FROM UNIT
			OFFICERS / OTHER RANKS : 27 / 771	OFFICERS / OTHER RANKS : 15 / 106
	29th		Aeroplane smash in morning about 0420 near A Coy's area. Both occupants killed - C.O. & Adjt. round billets. New G.O.C. Div. & Brigadier visit Battn. C.O.'s Conference with all Officers. Strength of Battn. 27 Officers - 771 OR	
	30th		Battalion prepare to move to new area at Finet Baggage Waggons move off at 0800 with Advance Party - Lieut. Telfer + 45 OR. Second load at 1200 Battalion moved off at 1500, pass starting point at 1600. Arrive at New Area about 1800	
			STRENGTH OF UNIT	DETACHED FROM UNIT
			OFFICERS / OTHER RANKS : 27 / 771	OFFICERS / OTHER RANKS : 15 / 106

J. Agnes Major
Cmdr. 5th Bn. A.&S.H.

RAID ORDERS
by Lieut-Col. C.L. Barlow D.S.O.
Commdg 5th Battn. A & S Highrs.

June 1918

1 INFORMATION — Rd. MAROEUIL 1.20.000
(a) The enemy are reported to have a post at T23d.7.1 covering the approach via HUDSON SAP to his front line.
(b) The enemy's wire in this vicinity is reported to be passable with the aid of good wire-cutters

2 INTENTION — On the night of _____ it is intended to raid the enemy trench in 23 D.7.2. in order to obtain
(a) Prisoners
(b) obtain identification
(c) inflict Casualties

Troops will withdraw immediately (a) or (b) has been obtained, failing this, 10 minutes after entering the enemy's trench.

(3) FORCE TO BE EMPLOYED — 2 Platoons
O.C. Raid
O.C. Raiding Platoon
O.C. Supporting Platoon
(a) One platoon (less Lewis Guns) Lt _____ Raiding Platoon
(b) " " (Complete) " _____ Covering Platoon

Strength of sections – 1 N.C.O. & 6 O.R.

(4) OBJECTIVE Enemy post at T.23.d.7.1. and his front line from point of entry T23d 75.20 southwards to T23d.75.15.

(5) POSITION OF ASSEMBLY – HUDSON TRENCH T23.C.45/05
POSITION OF DEPLOYMENT – IMMEDIATELY EAST of GAP in WIRE T23C 50/10

(6) HOUR OF ASSEMBLY – ZERO hour – 15 minutes

(7) DISPOSITION A. Raiding Platoon
B. Covering Platoon

A 1 Advance from position of Deployment at Zero + minutes
2 Compass bearing from position of assembly to point of entry in enemy wire 84° true.
3 Raiding party will file out through our own wire at Zero + 5 minutes.
4 Formation to be adopted will depend on the nature of the ground and darkness
5 A screen of scouts supplied from H.Q. Scouts will precede Raiding Platoon
6 O.C. Raiding Platoon will be responsible for direction and pointing out to the Scouts the location of gaps to be cut in enemy's wire.

Raid Orders (Contd.)

7 DISPOSITION (contd.)

A

7. The Scouts will cut a gap through enemy's wire at a point to be indicated by O.C. Raiding Platoon. Hand wire-Cutters will be issued for this purpose. After the Raiding Platoon has passed through, the Scouts will improve the gap for the return journey.

8. Immediately the gap has been made in the enemy's wire, the Raiding Platoon will proceed as follows:—

9. One section (No.1 Rifle Section) will cross enemy's trench, turn SOUTHWARDS and endeavour to surprise and scupper enemy's Post at T.23.d.73.10.

10. One section (No.2 Bombers) will enter Enemy's Trench, turn NORTH, proceed along trench for two bays and there Cover the rear of Raiding Sections either from Enemy's Trench or from WINNIPEG ROAD.

11. One section (No.3. Moppers-up) accompanied by O.C. Raiding Platoon will enter enemy's trench, turn SOUTH and following up No.1 Section, will mop up all dug-outs found, as far as T.23.d.73.10. (a distance of about 100 yards)

12. One section (No.4) will be with O.C. Raid at the entrance to the gap to be used as circumstances dictate.

13. On Completion of operation Raiding Platoon will re-assemble in HUDSON TRENCH

B

1. The supporting platoon under Lieut   will immediately follow the Raiding Platoon through our own wire.

2. Sections of the Covering Platoon will advance and take up position as follows:—

No.1 Section		T.23.d. 30/70
" 2 "	(astride Sap)	T.23.d. 30/75
" 3 "		T.23.b. 45/18
" 4 "		T.23.b. 43/40

    O.C. Covering Platoon will be with No.3 Section

Raid Orders (Cont'd)

-3-

DISPOSITION (Cont'd)

B
3. The Covering platoon will protect the flanks and the withdrawal of the Raiding Platoon, and deal energetically with any hostile parties attempting to outflank or interfere with the operations

4. As soon as the assaulting platoon has returned to our own trenches a rocket (Colour - Red) will be put up from HUDSON TRENCH. On this signal being given the supporting platoon will withdraw and re-assemble in HUDSON TRENCH.

(8) BOOTY   Prisoners Captured will be passed back to No. 4 Section, Raiding Platoon.

(9) WITHDRAWAL

The signal for withdrawal from Enemy's Trench will be 3 SHORT BLASTS on the whistle. If prisoners or identifications are secured the N.C.O. i/c of the Section securing same will immediately report to O.C. Raid, or assaulting platoon, with the prisoners or identifications. O.C. Raid or O.C. assaulting platoon will then sound the withdrawal signal, which will be repeated by the O.C. Raid or O.C. assaulting Platoon as the case may be.

In the event of no identification or prisoners being secured within 10 minutes of entering the enemy's trenches, O.C. Raid will sound the withdrawal signal which will be repeated by O.C. Assaulting Platoon. On this signal being given all sections of the Assaulting Platoon will close in on gap in enemy's wire under cover of supporting platoon. O.C. Assaulting Platoon will ensure that N.C.O. i/c of sections report all men of their respective sections present, before withdrawal from enemy's trench.

The Section Commander will be the last man of his section to leave the enemy's trenches. Similarly O.C. Assaulting Platoon will report to O.C. Raid prior to return journey.

10. SIGNAL COMMUNICATIONS - will be arranged by means of white tape which will be laid out by No. 1 Section, Raiding Platoon, up to the gap in the enemy's wire.

Raid Orders (Cont'd)
- 4 -

(11) **MEDICAL** - 4 S.Bs. with 2 stretchers and 2 blankets will accompany the Raiding Platoon, and move out in rear of No. 4 Section. The M.O. will arrange for an A.D.S. to be situated at T.22.B.9/2 and for a Relay Post of 4 S.Bs. and 2 Stretchers to be in readiness at this spot.

(12) **DRESS AND EQUIPMENT**

(a) Cap Comforters will be worn, one bandolier and two bombs will be carried by each man, field-dressings in possession. Kilt and apron will be worn. Bayonets will be fixed. Scouts will be armed with the bayonet only (no rifle). Each man of the bombing sections will carry 6 bombs and 1 "P" bomb.

(b) S. Bearers will carry full water-bottles. Scouts and each man of leading section (i.e. No.1. Sean. Raiding Platoon) will have wire-cutters attached to belt by string and carried in right-hand breast pocket. On no account will identity discs, letters, AB's 64 or diaries, shoulder numerals or anything else likely to give away the identity of this Unit, be carried.

(13) **DISTINGUISHING MARKS**

Raiding party will have their faces and hands blackened, thus every man met with in enemy's trenches with a white face will be readily identified as an enemy.

Personnel of each platoon will wear white armlets, 3" wide, on right arm, these to be securely fastened.

(14) **SILENCE**

Absolute silence will be observed throughout the operation.

(15) **PASSWORD** "HOG"

The regimental whistle - "The Campbells are Coming" will be used if required.

(16) **SYNCHRONISATION OF WATCHES** at Battn. H.Qrs 1800 Zero Day

(17) **ROLL-CALL** - Rolls will be prepared beforehand and checked as each man leaves the trench. All men of the Raiding Party will answer their names on return to the position of assembly.

Nominal Roll of Officers 1/5" A.S.H. at 30 June 1918

RANK	NAME		Coy	REMARKS	RANK	NAME		Coy	REMARKS
Lieut.(R.	Barlow	C.L.	HQ	Cmnndg.	Lieut.	McDonald	D.I.	B	
Major.	Agnew	J.	"	2' in Cmnd.	"	McLeod	H.	B	
Lieut.	Taylor	J.M.	"	of Adjt.	2/Lieut.	Hamilton	A.	B	
"	Fraser	W.A.	"	M.O.	"	Hamilton	W.B.	B	
2/Lieut.	Holroyd	C.W.	"	Lewis S. Off.	"	Galbraith		B	
"	Brown	R.M.	"	Pm.S.O.	Lieut.	Campbell	A.A.	C	
* "	Austin	R.	"	Transport Off.	2/Lieut.	Cameron	J.A.	"	
Lieut.	Hunnybun	W.G.W.	A		"	Allison	J.	"	
"	Telfer	A.C.	"		"	Robertson	G.C.A.	"	
2/Lieut.	Saunders	F.W.	"		"	Nixon		"	
"	Ritchie	W.S.	"		Capt.	Brown	R.	D	
"	Goodwin	J.G.	"		Lieut.	Fleming	D.	"	
"	Grant	D.M.	"		2/Lieut.	Watson	R.R.	"	
					"	Anderson	H.	"	
					"	Thom	J.S.	"	

P.T.O.

Nominal Roll of Officers not with Unit

RANK	NAME	Coy	HOW EMPLOYED	RANK	NAME	Coy	HOW EMPLOYED
2/Lieut	Hendry S.D.	B	General Course	2/Lieut.	Lindsay J.	A	Hospital
"	Martin P.C.	C	General Course	Capt.	Gibb J.S.	B	Leave.
"	Pryor F.R.	D	L.G. School	"	Campbell A.J.	HQ	"
"	Kennedy A.C.	A	Musketry School	"	King A.C.	C	Div. H.Q.
"	Langlands G.	HQ	Signalling "	"	Morrison F.	A	"
Lieut	Thomson G.R.	C	Infantry Course	Lieut	Morrison J.L.	A	"
Capt Q.M.	Watson W.J.	HQ	Hospital	Capt.	Deas A.O.	C	151st Bde. H.Q.
				2/Lieut.	Stewart J.M.	C	"

List of Casualties during June 1918

REG. NO.	RANK	NAME	COY	NATURE OF CASUALTY
S/19576	Pte.	Penman A.	A	Killed
275212	"	Gear R.	A	Wounded. Shrapnel rt. thigh, left leg
201261	"	McGinty P.	D	Wounded G.S.W. chest
276478	"	Sinclair J.	B	— " — sh.w chest
201681	"	Petrie A.	B	— " — sh.w L Shoulder, left fore-arm left leg
13238	L/Cpl.	McTaggart D.	D	— " — sh. back
200141	Pte.	Burke E.	D	— " — sh.w. R arm, R shoulder, R side L foot and neck
18252	"	Scott B.	D	— " — Sh.w. left shoulder
200102	"	Anderson M.	D	— " — Sh.w. head L arm thigh
202963	"	Brown A.	D	— " — sh.w. R thigh & L arms
201316	"	Hall W.	D	— " — Compound fracture L arm, sh.w. left thigh
S/20707	L/Cpl.	Todd C.	D	— " — sh.w. head
S/20706	Pte.	Sutherland G.	D	Killed
200327	"	Thomas R.	D	Killed

WAR DIARY or INTELLIGENCE SUMMARY

(Erase heading not required.)

Army Form C. 2118.

Place	Date 1918	Hour	Summary of Events and Information	Remarks and references to Appendices
St. Jean (nr) Major	July 1	11 a.m.	Battalion inspected by Brigadier, 103rd Brigade. On parade 550, all ranks. Lt. Col. Barton, D.S.O. in command. Brigadier complimented Battn. on smartness and appearance. Transport arrived by road from Poole Camp. Moved to bivy in afternoon.	
	2	11 a.m.	Battalion inspected by Corps Commander, General Jacob. Strength approximately same as yesterday. Major Stephens in command. Lt. Col. Barton, D.S.O. and Lt. Col. Jeffer proceeded to U.K. on leave. Capt. L.V. Gill returned from leave in U.K. Major A.B. Hoskin joined from 149th D. of 142.	
	3	11.30 a.m.	Brigade inspected by Army Commander General Plumer. Strength on parade 25 officers 532 O.R. Major J. Haynes in command. Weatherald and Asst. Adjt. Royalls were decorated by Army Commander as a first Battalion, 1/5 Graham, 1/6 and Newton joined Battn.	
	4	10 a.m.–4 p.m.	Battalion on miniature range firing with B.A.R. A&B Coys at Battn. and Battalion runners with strings of shooting. Camps area thoroughly cleaned up.	
	5	noon	Major Agnew, Hoskins and Coy Commanders reconnoitred Regt L.A. sector, Busnes. A & B Coys at Battn. C & D on Coy training. Battn. Que. Vue Sec, PT & B.F.	
	6	8.30 a.m.	Lectures to entire Brigade. Leave allotment increased to 6 per original Batt. 16 troops from the Ex. General Footballers match. 2nd R.A.M.C. Rentz. Rainy. 2 gents each.	
	7	8.30 a.m.	Brigadier inspected camp. Battn. on tent work (feet, machine guns) Band & Corneille Concert. Lt. Cain arranged Lt. Weatherald O/C attached battn. apt in afternoon. Battalion marched to Busnecopin. Entrained this 1.30 entrained L Brus 3pm and marched to Corps H.Q. Busnes KT. G.P. Chakirs. Transport travelled by road, apt. at 7am. 26 Middlesex Batt. joined Battn.	

6.M.

Army Form C. 2118.

WAR DIARY
or
INTELLIGENCE SUMMARY

(Erase heading not required.)

Place	Date	Hour	Summary of Events and Information	Remarks and references to Appendices
W. of Meynuel	July 29 1918		"D" Coy in reserve by day, and at night in line with "A" Coy and patrolled to Hill 158 with view of gaining information on which to base a fresh attack at dawn. Lt Col Berkers D.S.O. from Canadian Field Cas Sty. Capt A.J. Campbell, Capt. R.J. Gill, Lt. W.I. Ritchie took over command. Lieut C. White, and Zeffs, 2/Lts Goodwin, Mathieson, Graham, Gabrielli (R.S.) Rowbotham (Q.O.M) and 11 O.Rs. wounded. Lieut C. White, and Zeffs, Kerr, Huntley and Longlands, and 193 O.Rs.	
	30		Day spent consolidating, attack having been postponed. Battn. HQrs gas shelled at 1.30 a.m.	
	31		Brigat Agnew proceeded to Details. Lt Col Gare Osborn received about particulars of attack on morning of 1st Aug. Line weaker Lieut Kennedy to hospital (gassed). Lt. Grant Ellis "A" (C.D. Patterson "B" F. W. Saunders "C" and Lieut Fleming "D" Coy. Proportion of rifle and magazines taken according to strength of Coys, reorganised into 2 Platoons each. Moved up to jumping-off positions after nightfall. "C", "D" & "B" Coys in front line. "A" in support. Battn. HQrs. in reserve Dug in behind railway. Rifle fire and pistols received from Bde and issued. German Very Light sets were in front or the Battn. rifles shelling C.O. gas round bombline. Approximate strength of Battn. 7 officers, 280 O.R.	

Noel Brown Captain
for O.C. 1/5 A & S H.

WAR DIARY
INTELLIGENCE SUMMARY

7. M
Salbury

Place	Date	Hour	Summary of Events and Information	Remarks and references to Appendices
	1916 August 1st	04.00	Intense Artillery Fire from 0400 - 0445. Zero altered to 0445. Barrage opened 0445, jumping 100 metres every 3 min. App. strength before attack 6 Officers — 200 O.R. plus M.O. Capt. Sanders killed and Capt. Grant wounded before reaching Hill 158 S. of Beaumeux. Lieut. CQ Robertson wounded at Hill 158. Lieut Fleming left in command of attacking line going through Lieut-Col Badow DSO, Lieut Thurston & H.Qss. Coy. go round left of Hill. Hill 158 Captured at Second attempt — 4 Officers (including Bn. Commander & Adjt) and 40 OR taken prisoners, and about 10 machine guns captured. Battalion pushed on up the ridge, but held up by intense Machine Gun fire from 3 sides Lieut-Col Badow DSO. — RSM Monteith, CSM MacNab and 30 more, were killed during this period Col Coulson KOSB offered to hand French our men. Lieut Fleming Commanding Battalion. News of French Division pushing through us and pushing on, but we have to capture our whole objective before they will do so. — Small attack at 7pm & objective gained Boche Barrage comes down at 9 p.m. — Shells and Machine gun fire App Strength of Battn. — 2 Officers and 130 O.R. plus M.O.	
	2nd		Clothing and Baggage dead at about 148 (Map Ref: EN-ARD/S9) just East of Beauvineux Service by Padres at 3 p.m. French pushing through — Cavalry and infantry. Then lost touch with enemy, who was retiring along war	

WAR DIARY or INTELLIGENCE SUMMARY

Army Form C. 2118.

Place	Date	Hour	Summary of Events and Information	Remarks and references to Appendices
In the Field	August 2nd		Orders to get ready to move to a back area. Suddenly cancelled and orders issued to prepare to go forward in support of French Division. M.T. Transport ordered up to BEUGNEUX. French Division concentrating at BEUGNEUX. A few HV shells over. Very wet night. Rum issued and very acceptable.	
	3rd		Troops pouring into BEUGNEUX area and passing forward along the roads — Artillery, Balloons, etc. Definite orders to move to the British Zone on 4th inst. Congratulations all round. "Quaeque" specially distinguished for Croix de Guerre. Brigadier General comes round the lines. Received Croix de Guerre from French, presented by Gen. Nicholson 34th Div. Capt. Nairn "B" Coy. recommended for " Lieut. Y. Lunny & Capt. Nairn to B.H.Q. Wet night. Total strength — 4 Officers and 250 OR. (including M.O. Transport, R.Q.M.S, M.S's staff) hint Taylor from Limestock, own Offr's duties. Lunny from General Menzin.	
	4th		Ordered to move in morning by bus. Transport leave by road at 8 a.m. March off 8.15 a.m. — 3 Officers – 210 OR. (including M.O. & Q.M.S) Embus on main road, east of OUTCHY–de–VILLE, near original jumping–off place (Adjt. buried here hurriedly). Buses leave about 10 a.m. via PLESSIN – HELEN – BLANZY – LONGPONT – LARGNY – VEZ – CREPY – NANTEUIL – to MARCHÉMORET. Billeted there. Details from VEZ rejoined Battalion.	

WAR DIARY or INTELLIGENCE SUMMARY

Army Form C. 2118.

Place	Date	Hour	Summary of Events and Information	Remarks and references to Appendices
In the Field	August 5th to 6th		At MARCHÉ MORET Battalion moved by train from DAMMARTIN (St. MARD) Station to British Zone. H.Q.–C.–D. Coys left MARCHÉMORET at 3-30 p.m. Marching to DAMMARTIN, arriving station 5-30 p.m. – Tea drawn and rations for 7th instant issued. Tea supplied en route at 11 p.m. and in forenoon of 7th. Route via outskirts of PARIS – BOULOGNE – CALAIS – NORD line to REXPOEDE. A – B Coys "loading party" (for Brigade) at DAMMARTIN. 'A' Coy – 1 NCO – 6 men on guard during railway journey.	
	7th		Detrained at REXPOEDE 9 p.m. and marched off to WORMHOUDT, billeted there in farm buildings	
	8th		Draft of 18 men from U.K. joined today, also draft of 44 men from leave. Captain Thurston C.R. – 2/Lieut. Theam, rejoined from courses. Capt. Shearer R.E. and 2/Lieut. Carmichael rejoined from Hospital.	
	9th		Draft of 170 from U.K. via Base, arrived — also draft of 200.	
	10th		Battalion parades – 8.30 to 12.15 – under Coy. arrangements. Recent Gunners under 2/Lieut. Cameron at Bn.H.Q. Lieut. McKenzie D.K. joined Battalion and posted to A Coy. Lieut. Archer. R.G. " " " C " Capt. Shearer J.T. " " " B " 2/Lieut. Thesson J. (Q.C.H.) " " " C " 2/Lieut. Thornton " to U.K. on 14 days leave Presentation of French decorations to Officers and O.R. in WORMHOUDT today.	

Army Form C. 2118.

WAR DIARY
or
INTELLIGENCE SUMMARY
(Erase heading not required.)

Instructions regarding War Diaries and Intelligence Summaries are contained in F. S. Regs., Part II. and the Staff Manual respectively. Title Pages will be prepared in manuscript.

Place	Date	Hour	Summary of Events and Information	Remarks and references to Appendices
In the Field	August 11th		Divine Service. Capt. Brown R. (M.C) rejoined from ETAPLES — 10 A.M. 2/Lieut Orr — 2/Lieut Hamilton. N.B. rejoined from Courses. 2/Lieut Hamilton A. resigned from Hospital today 2/Lieut Thomson D. posted to 'C' Coy. Capt. Lyfe W. joined today & posted to 'A' Coy. For duty 14-8-18	
	12th		Draft of 229 men from U.K. joined today. 2/Lieut R. McCarmichael to Bombing Course — MILLAIN — II Corps School. Parades — 8.30 to 12.30 — 2 to 3 p.m. Sigs. A.G. gunners under Bn Officers at Bn. HQ. 9-30 a.m.	
	13th		Battalion moved to School Camp this afternoon. Left WORMHOUDT at 7.30 a.m. Full marching order. Warm weather and roads dusty — fully 3 hours march.	
	14th		2/Lieut Hamilton N.B. to II Corps Signal School — MILLAIN. Lieut D.P. Macdonald to U.K. on 14 days leave. Coy Parades as usual — range firing etc.	
	15th		Major Thorburn O.B. to 52nd Divisional HQ for duty today. 2/Lieut Anderson H. & T.34 L.T.M.B. for duty today. Above the effective strength of unit 15-8-18. Captain Brown R. (M.C) in Command of Battalion. Grounded as usual.	
	16th		Battalion moved to DIRTY BUCKET Area "O" Camp, moving off 8.45 a.m. Arrived at new Camp 11 a.m and billeted in huts. Battn Transport at DROOGENTAK farm also Q.M. Stores to date 30-7/18. 2/Lieut Hamilton A. to hospital today. Lieut Taylor appointed Adjutant — 2/Lieut Rome D. joined for duty and posted to 'C' Coy. 2/Lieut. Allan Q. joined for duty and posted to 'B' Coy	

Army Form C. 2118.

WAR DIARY
or
INTELLIGENCE SUMMARY.
(Erase heading not required.)

Place	Date	Hour	Summary of Events and Information	Remarks and references to Appendices
In the Field	August 17th		Busy day. Specialist training – Gas and Steady drill in forenoon	
	18th		Captains (Brown) Thomas & Thomson, Lieut Walton & Cameron, had reconnaissance of front line. Divine Service	
	19th		Lieut R.M. Dunn proceeded to UK on leave. Parades as usual, particularly Gas Drill – theatrical & practical 2/Lieut Carmichael J.G. joined today and posted to 'C' Coy 2/Lieut Scott D.C. " " B " 2/Lieut McCance J. " " B " Dinner party under Lieut Thompson proceeded to line at YPRES	
	20th		Battalion paraded in forenoon – Same arrangements as 19th – moved off in Battle Order at 7-30 p.m. – intervals of 100 yards between sections – and 200 yards between Coys. Hon. Lieut. J. Quill & Shackleton (9th LNL) joined today, also 2/Lieut O. Wilson Arrangement of Coys in line – A LEFT – C RIGHT – B SUPPORT – D RESERVE	
	21st		Enemy shelling YPRES. Quiet in front line.	
	22nd		Strength of Battalion – 25 Officers – 845 O.R.	

WAR DIARY
or
INTELLIGENCE SUMMARY.
(Erase heading not required.)

Army Form C. 2118.

5 August H

Place	Date	Hour	Summary of Events and Information	Remarks and references to Appendices
In the Field	August 23rd		2/Lieut Thorson OR to II Army Signal School for Course. Dump shelled. 1 man killed. Hut shelled with gas. Lieut Humphries and 11 men gassed.	
	24th		2/Lieut Cameron to DROGLAND for Camp Cmdt Course. Lieut. Humphries and 2 men 'C' Coy to Hosp (gassed). Lieut. W. Campbell from Hospital today. Draft of 27 (Canada Hospital Leave) arrived. Divine Services. Lieut Coy relief. 'D' relieved 'A' on right "B" relieved 'C' on right. Major Ogmore from leave 24/8/18, and assumed Command of Battalion 25/8/18 at Lieut. Col.	
	25th		50 O.R. from Details to 209 Field Coy R.E. for temporary duty, and rejoined unit 28/8/18. Lieut. Fleming to U.K. on 14 days leave. 2/Lieut Scott to Hospital (sick). Lieut Twaites, 2/Lieut Cunningham & 2/Lieut Ritchie joined, also draft of 13	
	26th		Supports & Reserve shelled with gas in evening. Quiet day in line. Day patrol to Gordon House. Advance party from 33rd Rodies (R.B.) arrived.	
	27th		Battalion relieved in YPRES by R.B. Moved back & billeted in BRAKE Camp (DIRTY BUCKET)	
	28th		2/Lieut. McGregor joined for duty and posted to 'A' Coy. Battalion cleaned up & rested throughout day.	
	29th		Relieved by 14th WILTS (14th Div) and marched in evening to WIPPENHOEK, via POPERINGHE &	
	30th		Lieut. Col Ogmore and Coy Commdrs reconnoitred SCHERPENBERG area. Battalion under orders to move off at short notice.	
	31st		At WIPPENHOEK awaiting orders. Marched to RENINGHELST 1 p.m. — 21 Off. — 592 O.R. Ward to GORDON Road position 8-30 p.m. Showering & very wet. Took up position in depth A and C in front, B in support, D in Reserve. Capt. Brown to Details — 128 O.R.	

(signature)

WAR DIARY
or
INTELLIGENCE SUMMARY
(Erase heading not required.)

Army Form C. 2118.

Place	Date	Hour	Summary of Events and Information	Remarks and references to Appendices
In the Field	Sept 1st		"B" – "D" and half of "A" Coy carried rations to Battalions in front. In KEMMEL area.	
	2		In Reserve. Quiet. Orders. S.R. and K.O.S.B. make advance. Hostile Shelling but not much in our area. Guide took 1/7 Wellings forward. S.R. – K.O.S.B. Very cold at night.	
	3		2/Lieut BR Watson to UK on leave. Battn. relieved at 5-30, & marched to Pte CLYTTE, & to own band supper. Bridges. Cmne arrived, and lumined orders for move postponed. 2/Lieut Cameron and 7 men wounded by shell.	
	4		Battn. moved back to KEMMEL area. At midnight occupied area at 4 Bullets. Shelled for an hour – 0200 – 0300. Casualties 6. Battn. settled down behind ridge. Lieut. McDonald & Thomson back from leave. 2/Lt Caldwell joined for duty. Quiet there. 2/Lt Watson transferred to 10th Battn A & S Highrs.	
	5		2/Lieut Allen i/c Euacuard Party – then cancelled. Moved at 8-30 to SCHERPENBERG Line – M122. Quiet move. Trouble with Artillery. Lieut. McGlashan joined for duty. Prospers NI in front.	
	6		Brigade Ops called. Battn. cleaning up.	
	7		Cog on training – 9–1, and 2–3. A, C, & D Coys on working parties. Heavyrain. Lieut. Campbell on reconnaissance.	
	8		Major Wilson assumed of troops over Command vice Major Orpen. R.O. un arrived and later proceeded with Advance Post to STEENVOORDE. Coys clothing. Very heavy rain. Battn. relieved by Cheshires. Marched to E. of STEENVOORDE. Very good march. Coys into THQ in fine-sand were comfortable.	
	9		2/Lieut Bennie assumed of posted to C Coy Pcints Macleod & Hamilton (NB) assigned, also Capt Brown & 2/Lieut Carmichael from Details.	

Army Form C. 2118.

WAR DIARY
or
INTELLIGENCE SUMMARY.
(Erase heading not required.)

Instructions regarding War Diaries and Intelligence Summaries are contained in F. S. Regs., Part II. and the Staff Manual respectively. Title pages will be prepared in manuscript.

Place	Date	Hour	Summary of Events and Information	Remarks and references to Appendices
In the Field	Sept 10		C. & D. Coys. left by rail at 2 p.m. Remainder at 3 p.m. Arrived at ST MOMELIN — 6 p.m. Marched via MOULLE, EPERLEQUES — to BAYENGHEM. The Guides Arrived at billets midnight. Tea for men. Battalion compact and in bivouacs etc.	
	11th		Battn. cleaning up. A Coy. bathed & received clean clothing. Kit inspections. Transport arrived 9 p.m. CO lectured Officers and NCO's. Brigr. Gen. & Staff Capt. called in afternoon. Heavy Showers. Coys. re-assembling.	
	12th		Battn. Parade — A & D Coys. on range. B & C Coys. on Platoon Training. Brigr. Gen. on training ground & arrived at range.	
	13th		Weather cold and wet. A & D Coys. doing Artillery Formations. B & C Coys. at Range also L Gunners under Capts. Iyffe. Brigr. Gen. round.	
	14th		Church service and Presentation of medals in Tomorrow at EPERLEQUES. Lieut. Carmichael Hamilton off to U.K. for Indian Army. Lieut. Fleming + Hungerbr. arrived. Lieut. T. Jones (O.C.M.)	
	15th		Brigade Scheme of Communications. Lieuts Caldwell, Rose, and Allan — to crosss. Lieut. McPhedran to H.Q. Coy. D Coy. on field firing range.	
	16th		Commanding Officer visited Lines. "A-B-C & D Coys on range and doing Scheme P.G. Gunners under Capt. Iyffe.	
	17th		Bright day. Received Orders for Move.	
	18th		CO's Conference. Capt. Brown to R.A.F. A Coy. at Field firing. Orders for move Cancelled. Lieut. McKenzie from Gas Course. CO's Conference at night. Demonstration at 19th Corps School. B.9.0. & T.9.0. with advance Party to French Bank	

WAR DIARY or INTELLIGENCE SUMMARY

Army Form C. 2118.

Place	Date	Hour	Summary of Events and Information	Remarks and references to Appendices
In the field Sept	19		Training – "A" & "D" Coys – Coy schemes. "B" & "C" Coys'-manoeuv: Orders rec'd for move to line	
	20		2/Lieut Puckett & MK Kinnon report for duty – C.O. visited front line – Batt. moved from BAYENGHEM to WATTEN & entrain 3·30 p.m. Reached ABEELE 6·30 p.m. & billeted in transit Camp	
	21		Transport left 2 p.m. for forward area. Details (5 Officers & 130 OR) left for Détails Camp. Batt. entrained 5·30 p.m. (20 Officers & 581 OR) for line. Detrained at HALLEBAST – relieved 18 K.R.R. (VIERSTRAAT switch) – Relief complete 11·40 p.m. C.O. around line – slight shelling around Batt H.Q.	
	22nd		A & B Coys in front line – C & D Coys in support. Posts & Craters visited. Lieut Fleming to Hospital	
	23rd		Coy reliefs – 2/Lieut Watson returned from UK leave	
	24th		C.O.s Conference at H.Q. B.G.C. & C.O. around line – 2 casualties. New Zealand Honours list to Bde H.Q. Bde in consolidation of position. Orders W Coy 8 S.R. relieved C. Coy 5th A & S.H.	
	25th		Wet morning. Slight shelling of area – Secret orders for C Coy arrive. D Coy relieved B Coy in front line	
	26th		Capt. R. Ashcroft to R.A.F. Daylight patrol from B Coy. Verified previous information 90 wire & ground in front – L/c Wilkinson in charge of patrol	
	27th		Capt. Lyffe transferred to 8 A & S H. Batt. H.Q. moved to D Coys H.Q. 8 p.m. – C.O. Conference – Orders for Body on Operation order. advance completed	
	28th		Batt. H.Q. moved to Craters 4 a.m. – Enemy shelling commenced 3·20 a.m. – Attack commenced 3·30 a.m. – Red Chateau taken by A Coy 6·30 a.m. (8 prisoners) – D Coy on left held up by M.G. fire – reinforced by B Coy at 10 a.m. Batt. line at noon was N & S. through GRAND Bois to Molthem Brickstacks. Bn H.Q. in centre of GRAND BOIS at 2 p.m. – Got in touch with K.O.S.B. at 3 p.m. – Line advanced 3·30 p.m.	

WAR DIARY
INTELLIGENCE SUMMARY

Army Form C. 2118.

Place	Date	Hour	Summary of Events and Information	Remarks and references to Appendices
In the Field	Sept 28th (Cont)		"B" Coy storms ZERO House taking a few prisoners — 2 A Tank guns — 1 T.M. (Granaten-Werfer) and 1 M.G. Right held up by M.G. fire on WYTSCHAETE RIDGE. Lieut. McGrath killed — 14 OR killed and 47 wounded. 23 OR missing. 8th Scottish Rifles advanced at 5-30 am. A + B Coys. 5th A+S.H. at 5.45 a.m. acting as supports — "D" Coy 5th A+S.H + "W" Coy 8th S.R. in reserve. Very slight opposition met with. Battn. H.Q. direceuve Coys. moved forward at noon + Battn. took up positions in depth as follows:- "A" Coy on right in ROSE WOOD — "B" Coy on left to WYCLIFFE Trench. "W" Coy S.R. + "D" Coy A+S.H. in Support 500 yards behind. Battn. H.Q. at DENYS WOOD —	
	29th		Moved back at 7 pm to ZERO House — Tiptel darkness — Sometime moving we contend. Still raining + very cold. Coys. re-organising. Captured enemy material of tents + Transport loads + Priest Thom regains from U.K. leave. Capt. Hutchison from 10th Corps School lines. attached — Priest Kerr M.C. from 8th A+S.H. reported + took over Command of "D" Coy from Lieut. Dow.	
	30th		Strength with Battalion — 15 Officers — 338 OR	

WAR DIARY
INTELLIGENCE SUMMARY

Army Form C. 2118.

1/5 A&SH

103/34

Place	Date	Hour	Summary of Events and Information	Remarks and references to Appendices
Zext House	1/10/18	08.00	Strength with Battalion. 15 Officers, 338 O.R. Marched to Zandvoorde. Arrived 11.00	
Zandvoorde	2/10/18	10.00	Marched off and lay in open at German Cemetery. 19.00 Marched via America Corner, and took over front line from 1/4th & 1/8th L.N.L. to left of Werwicq. 23.30 Relief completed. B Coy in front line. 'A' & 'D' Coys in support. Scotch Rifles on right. K.O.S.B. in support.	
Werwicq	3/10/18		B Coy extended their line to left. A Coy took over from Middlesex in front line on left of B Coy. Heavy shelling 23.00 to 03.00, 4/10-18.	
"	4/10/18		America Corner shelled in afternoon. 2/Lt. Holroyd reported to Battalion.	
"	5/10/18		Headqrs. The Gar. shelled. Relieved by 1/6th Inni Killings. Bivouacked in area near Kruiseick.	
Kruiseick	6/10/18		Men in open without cover. Very cold. Watches adjusted to Winter time. 2/Lt. Allen reported from course. 2/Lt. Main, Longbow Henderson (reinforcements) reported from Base. Coys. washing and re-organising.	
"	7/10/18		Coys on tactical schemes. 2/Lt. Holroyd and 9 O.R. to details for Lewis Gun class. Officer reinforcements America. 2/Lt. Mercer, 2/Lts. Burgh, Bleath, McNaughten reported from Base, and 2/Lt. Caldow from course. Shelling and gas.	
"	8/10/18		Casualties at Transport lines at Zandvoorde. during night.	
"	9/10/18		B & D Coys. wiring and digging support line at night. 'A' Coy on scheme under supervision of Capt. Trelawn. 2/Lt. Watson to hospital. Lt. Fraser (RAMC) to W. On leave. Lt. McCall (American Army) joined bn. Lts. Baker, Slaney & McKenzie.	
"	10/10/18		E & D Coys. moved H.Q. and Coys further back from our batteries. Gas shelled at night.	
"	11/10/18		2/Lt. Snitcher, McNaughten & McKenzie to Transport lines. 2/Lt. McRae reconnoitring positions in front. Battalion at baths. Capt. Smith gone to Transport lines. Capt. J. Shearer to W.K. on leave.	
"	12/10/18		Coys. moved to new area, 1000 yds. away. CO., Adjt. and Coy Commanders made reconnaissance of immediate front.	

WAR DIARY
or
INTELLIGENCE SUMMARY.
(Erase heading not required)

Army Form C. 2118.

Place	Date	Hour	Summary of Events and Information	Remarks and references to Appendices
Kruisstraat	13.10.18		I/O Moving to Bde. as liaison officer. Completed operation orders. 'C' Coy arrived from Reninghelst. 5 Officers, 140 O.R. Strength with Battalion 21 Officers, 4/14 O.R.	
	14.10.18	01.00	Marched off to point of assembly 1500 yds behind Pickrue. Order of battle. Scottish Rifles right, KOSB. Left, 5th A.S.H in support. A+C Coy in front. Batt. H.Q. with S.R. in pill box. B+D Coy in support. Attack commenced 05.35 with heavy barrage. Enemy put down counter barrage at 05.00. Smoke and fog retards advance. Batt. H.Q. moved to Anclien Farm. 10.00 and got in touch with B+D Coy. Liason difficult. A+C Coy moved up just forward of Batt. H.Q. Battery of field guns checked advance. L/. Macdonald, 1/Lt. Swiper & Black wounded in afternoon. 21.00 Final objective gained. Casualties, 70 O.R.	
Menin	15.10.18		Batt. H.Q. moved forward to pill box E. of wire belt. W.E returns wounded. Patrols started up Canal at Marathon Bridge. Menin at 07.00. Battn took up Liver [Line] line in afternoon 'C'+'B' Coys in front. D+'A' Coy in support. Batt. H.Q at Railway Triangle. 22.00 Posts established on river bank on W. side. Draft of 36 joined. Strength Officers 16. O.R 403	
	16.10.18		1/Lt. Thomson and 4 O.R. crossed Canal and reconnoitred ground towards Hallumn capturing 1 machine gun. 04.30 Patrol made bridge across Canal with barges, established post on S. side of river, and returned, reporting ground clear of enemy. Congratulatory wire received from G.O.C. on patrols good work. Capt: I. H. Young (M.C) reported to Batt. from Transport Lines. 16.00 Disposition 'B' Coy Bde. front on N bank of canal, 'C' Coy defensive flank facing S. on N bank of canal. A' + D' Coys in support. Several casualties with shell fire. Casualties to date from 14th 5 Officers, 86 O.R. Capt + Adjt. J. Mor. Taylor wounded, but remained on duty.	

WAR DIARY
INTELLIGENCE SUMMARY

Army Form C. 2118.

Place	Date	Hour	Summary of Events and Information	Remarks and references to Appendices
Menin area	17.10.18		Battn. crossed Lys and took up outpost line, 1000 yds beyond 23 vo. Withdrew. Battn. H.Q. moved to Tent Farm. Coys at hand. Enemy aircraft bombing at night	
	18.10.18		Battn. rested all day, and preparing to reorganise when orders to move arrived. Transport came up to farm not HQ. 2/Lt. Shearer to UK on leave	
	19.10.18		Battn. crossed Lys at Ruddy Bridge, marched through Lauwe to Knocke 16 vo. Arrived and billeted in houses and farms. Adjt at Bde ro A'Echelon. Battn. on 1 hour's notice. Major Agnew and Q.M. party rejoined. 2/Lt. Hobrough ordered to rejoin with details	
Knocke area	20.10.18		2/Lts. Oliphant & Stretton with draft of 107 casuals arrived. Coys working and reorganising. Battn. on 4 hours notice. Lt. Hennepin to hospital. Lt. McKenzie in Command of 'A' Coy. 2/Lt Archer and 2/Lt Porrington to 'A' Coy. Lewis guns cleaned and rifles inspected by Armourer.	
	21.10.18		G.O.C. inspected billets.	
	22.10.18		Coys during schemes. Lecture by Capt Young to Officers C.O. and Adjt round Coys. Visit by BGC. 2/Lt. Brock died of wounds.	
	23.10.18		2/Lt Hobrough with hand and 93 details, reported from Abeele Coy. on outpost patrol work. C.O. lectured on Consolidation.	
	24.10.18		2/Lt Ritchie to course. Capt G.R. Thomson to UK on leave. 09.40 Battn. moved off. 13:00 arrived E. of Bollington. Area overcrowded, but men under cover in farms by 21.00. Strength Officers 27, O.R. 372. Capt Rorke (M.C.) from 3rd Battn. and 2/Lt Lowe from course arrived. Coys reorganising and men resting.	
	25.10.18		12 O.R. left for X Corps Demonstration Platoon	

WAR DIARY
or
INTELLIGENCE SUMMARY

(Erase heading not required.)

Army Form C. 2118.

Place	Date	Hour	Summary of Events and Information	Remarks and references to Appendices
Hazel area	26.10.18		Battalion marched to St Anne area. Surplus stores sent to Laune. Capt Mackie takes over command of 'A' Coy. Billeted in farms.	
St Anne area	29.10.18	10.30	Battalion marched off, via Cruxbrai, Harlebeke where a halt was made for lunch to Huttete. Billeted in factory and farms. Major Agnew off to Paris on leave. Strength 29 Officers. 702 ORanks.	
Huttete	28.10.18	14.00	Received Operation Orders for move. A, B, & HQ Coys moved off 15.30. C & D Coy 16.00, and relieved 2nd K.O.S.B. at Heestert. Heytberg (reserve area) KOSB on right, S Rifles on left (reserve). Casualties 4 ORanks wounded. Strength in line 21 Officers 591 ORanks.	
Heytberg	29.10.18		M.O. back from leave. S.Officer (reinforcement) arrived at Details. Batteries all around, out own shelled.	
"	30.10.18		Completed Operation Orders for advance. Capt Webb joined and took command of 'C' Coy. Heytberg heavily shelled. 23.59 moved to Battle HQ. 'A' Coy attached to KOSB, 'B' Coy to Scotch Rifles. Advance continued. KOSB on right, S Rifles on left. Brigade objective gained by 11.00. Battalion HQ moved to Hevibeck at 10.00. 15.00 Battalion went forward to Bergstraat. Joint HQ with KOSB.	
"	31.10.18		'B' & 'C' Coys took up position on railway embankment W. of factory at Anseghem. D & A Coys in support. 'B' Coy patrol under Lt. Zunder occupied Hills T73 and T7hr near Broekkant. B Coy pushed forward to occupy positions. Casualties 1 OR killed, wounded Capt Mackie, ⅔ Lieut Oliphant and 43 OR. Strength of Battalion — in line Officers 20 ORanks 420 at details do. 13 do 213	

Argwisoy. Lord G. Glouadicea.
Lon by A.S.

Instructions regarding War Diaries and Intelligence
Summaries are contained in F. S. Regs., Part II.
and the Staff Manual respectively. Title pages
will be prepared in manuscript.

Army Form C. 2118.

WAR DIARY
INTELLIGENCE SUMMARY.
(Erase heading not required.)

Vol 8

10.M.

Place	Date	Hour	Summary of Events and Information	Remarks and references to Appendices
BOSCHKANT	11/11/18	0400	In the early morning 'C' Coy patrolled up to the top of Hill 83 (K20 c.5.2) and finding it unoccupied by the enemy held farms at the top of the Hill farming Western end of village of BOSCHKANT (K26.6) until relieved by French troops about 09:00 hours. 'C' Coy then moved to a farm on the hillside to reorganize and await orders. Shortly after noon orders were received to hand over from 5th K.O.S.B. at GYSELBRECHTEGHEM and advance between the 31st Division on right and French troops on left at 13:36 hours. 'C' Coy was in position by 13:25 hours and as 31st Division had already started it moved off at once. Company's final objective was the junction of French & 31st Division about 3 kilos EAST of GYSELBRECHTEGHEM. 'C' Coy advanced in Artillery formation and cleared the villages of BLAARHOEK and BOSCHKANT. (K27.) The enemy rifle fire was encountered but the area was in full view from enemy balloons on the SOUTH bank of the SCHELDT and some shelling was encountered. Patrols reached final objective by 15:00 hours and got into touch with both 31st Division and French. American troops could also be seen well in front and half left. The order to withdraw was received about 17:30 hours and Company marched back to STEENHOEK. The whole action cost only 2 slight casualties from shell fire. Bn. Hq at Chapel J36-4.	Ref Belgium & Part of France Sheet /29 1/40,000. Apple I.

WAR DIARY
INTELLIGENCE SUMMARY.
(Erase heading not required.)

Army Form C. 2118.

Instructions regarding War Diaries and Intelligence Summaries are contained in F. S. Regs., Part II. and the Staff Manual respectively. Title pages will be prepared in manuscript.

Place	Date	Hour	Summary of Events and Information	Remarks and references to Appendices
	1/11/18		This was the last occasion on which the Battalion was under fire. Capt R. Ker M.C. to Lewis Gun Course.	
STEENHOEN	2/11/18		Capt Welch took over command of A Coy. 2/Lt. Carmichael assumed command of C Coy. 2/Lt. Kennedy and Scott reported from hospital. Capt Fyfe took over command of D Coy.	
	3/11/18		Battalion marched to BISSEGHEM via COURTRAI. 2/Lt. Quaile, Mackie and Gardiner joined Battalion. Distance 14 miles. Good marching as one fell out.	
BISSEGHEM	4/11/18		Battalion employed generally cleaning up.	
	5/11/18		Company Training.	
	6/11/18		No training owing to Divisional Interior Economy. 2/Lt Sinclair & McKinnon rejoined from Courses.	
	7/11/18		Company Training. Major George rejoined from PARIS Leave.	
	8/11/18		Battalion marched to HALLUIN via WEVELGHEM. Distance 8 miles. Lt Austin proceeded on leave to U.K., 2/Lt McKinnon acting Transport Officer	
HALLUIN	9/11/18		Company Training	
	10/11/18		Church Parade. Capt S.R. Thomson & Capt T. Skinner M.C. rejoined from U.K. leave. Received message at 21-15 hours that Armistice between ALLIES and GERMANY had been signed. Battalion turned out with Pipe Band and marched through the town. Rockets and flares sent up from aerodromes and searchlights	

WAR DIARY or INTELLIGENCE SUMMARY.

Army Form C. 2118.

(Erase heading not required.)

Place	Date	Hour	Summary of Events and Information	Remarks and references to Appendices
	10/11/18		Worked in all directions.	
	11/11/18		Bugles sound to celebrate the signing of the Armistice. Brigade Commander called for 3 cheers for the King. Demonstrations noised from all ranks.	
	12/11/18		Company training. Draft of 20 O.R. arrived. Major Agnew proceeded to U.K. on 6 months leave of abs.	
	13/11/18		Company training. Capt. Nocket proceeded to U.K. to Lieut. W. McEwing's assumed command of 'A' Coy. 2/Lt A. Hamilton from Hosp.	
	14/11/18		Battalion marched via MOUSCRON to DOTTIGNES. Distance 11 miles. Strength 34 Officers 735 O.R.	(Ref. Sheet TOURNAI 1G. 1/100,000)
	15/11/18		Battalion marched via ESPIERRES across the SCHELDT through HERINNES to MOLEMBAIX. Distance 12 miles.	
			2/Lt. Goodman to U.K. on Special Leave.	
	16/11/18		Battalion marched via CELUBES and WATTRIPONT to ST. SAUVEUR. Distance 12½ miles. Capt. Fyfe proceeded on leave to U.K. 2/Lt Thom assumed command of 'D' Coy. 2/Lt Ribbles from course. 2/Lt Sinclair joined Battalion from HALLUIN.	Map showing route followed by Battalion WANNEBECQ is attached. App No II
ST. SAUVEUR	17/11/18		Brigade paraded for Special Thanksgiving Service.	
	18/11/18		Battalion marched via ESCALETTE - LA MAMAIDE to WANNEBECQ. Distance 11 miles.	
WANNEBECQ	19/11/18		Commanding Officer - Lieut. Col. A.R.B. Wilson awarded D.S.O. Capt & Adj. T.McN. Taylor awarded M.C. Following other awards 2/Lt D. Thomson D.C.M. Capt & Adj. T.McN. = M.M. No. 208438 Corporal 2/Lt B. Thomson D.C.M. awarded M.C. Following other awards awarded M.M. = No. 208438 Corporal McFadyen D. 20736 Pte McMillan R. 14707 Pte Inns-Smith S.W. 19050 Pte Richard R. 23859 Pte Burgoyne T.	

Army Form C. 2118.

WAR DIARY
INTELLIGENCE SUMMARY
(Erase heading not required.)

Instructions regarding War Diaries and Intelligence Summaries are contained in F. S. Regs., Part II. and the Staff Manual respectively. Title pages will be prepared in manuscript.

Place	Date	Hour	Summary of Events and Information	Remarks and references to Appendices
HANNEBECQ	20/11/18		Draft of 30 O.R. and R.S.M. Gray reported. Company Training.	
"	21/11/18		Company Training. Strength 33 Officers 773 O.R. 2/Lt Burns rejoined from course.	
"	22/11/18		Company Training.	
"	23/11/18		Battalion Drill.	
"	24/11/18		Divine Service.	
"	25/11/18		No training owing to rain. Interior Economy.	
"	26/11/18		Battalion Route March. Lt. Anokin rejoined from U.K. Leave.	
"	27/11/18		Battalion Parade. Ceremonial Drill. 2/Lt. Shears from Leave & Hospital.	
"	28/11/18		Brigade Commander inspected Transport. Capt R. Kerr M.C. from U.K. Leave. Company Training.	
"	29/11/18		Brigade Commander inspected Brigade.	
"	30/11/18		St Andrew's Day. General Holiday. Battalion Sports. Capt Welch rejoined from U.K. Leave. Strength 36 Officers 748 O.R.	
			2/Lt. Dunn to Hospital.	

A.E. Wilson Lieut. Col.
Comdg. 2/15th Bn. Argyll & Sutherland Highlanders

WAR DIARY
INTELLIGENCE SUMMARY
(Erase heading not required.)

Army Form C. 2118.

5 A+SH Vol 9

Place	Date	Hour	Summary of Events and Information	Remarks and references to Appendices
WANNEBECQ	1/12/18	-	Battalion parade for Divine Service. Strength 40 Officers 847 O.R.	Bat TOURNAI/s Yam, ans Sgt BRUSSELS
"	2/12/5	-	Battalion Parade. Ceremonial Drill. Capt T.Sleaser L/W on special leave Lt Macleod L 103	9/100 am Shot NAMUR
"		-	Lects as Educational Officer.	9/100 am shewed attacked
"	3/12/5	-	No parade on account of rain. 2/Lt. T.B. Mackie appointed Bn. Demobilization Officer.	Shewed route followed by
"	4/12/5	-	Kit Inspection by Companies.	Shawn from BRUSSELS to ANSEL 4/5
"	5/12/5	-	Divisional Commander inspected Brigade. Brigade headed past Capt. D Fyfe + 2/Lt. Goodman returned from U.K. sounding Kings + Regimental Colours.	
"	6/12/5	-	Bn. Route March. Lt Arther L Divisional Reception Camp finding teams. Battalion Concert Party gave two performances in LESSINES. Commanding Officer Lt-Col. A.R.G.Wilson D.S.O.) awarded Croix de Guerre (Army).	
"	7/12/5	-	Battalion Parade h reserve colours.	
"	8/12/5	-	Divine Service. Following Officers L BRUSSELS on 48 hours leave: Lt. McKing's 2/Lt. McCrae. 2/Lt. Cunningham.	
"	9/12/8	-	Battalion Route March. Divisional Commander presented ribbon of award shown opposite each name to the following Officers + O.R. Lt-Col. A.R.G.Wilson D.S.O. - D.S.O. + Croix de Guerre Capt. + Adjt. J.M.Taylor. M.C. M.C. 2/Lt. D. Thomson. M.C. D.C.M. - M.C.	11.11

Army Form C. 2118.

WAR DIARY
or
INTELLIGENCE SUMMARY.
(Erase heading not required.)

Instructions regarding War Diaries and Intelligence Summaries are contained in F. S. Regs., Part II. and the Staff Manual respectively. Title pages will be prepared in manuscript.

Place	Date	Hour	Summary of Events and Information	Remarks and references to Appendices
VANNEBECQ.	9/11/18 (cont)		No.200488 Cpl. D. McFadyen M.M. — M.M. No.20736 Pte R. McMillan M.M. — M.M.	
			No.14704 Pte James Smith M.M. — M.M. No.19050 Pte R. Prichard M.M. — M.M.	
			No.23850 Pte T. Dugsdale M.M. — M.M.	
VANNEBECQ.	10/11/18		Battalion Parade. Ceremonial Drill. 'A' Coy beat 'D' Coy K.O.S.B. in final of Association Football Competition for Brigade Commanders Cup. (Score 1–0)	
	11/11/18		Very wet. Parades under Coy Arrangements. Lieut. D.K. McKenzie's leave to U.K. Col Bailey lectured in LESSINES – Subject "Relations of Labour & Capital after the war".	
	12/11/18		Battalion marched from VANNEBECQ to GRATY in pouring rain. Route LESSINES/CHISLEGHIEN. Distance 13 miles. No one fell out.	
GRATY	13/11/18		No parades. Bn. resting.	
	14/11/18		Battalion marched to NAAST. Route SOIGNIES/ROEULX. Distance 12 miles	
	15/11/18		Battalion parade for Divine Service.	
	16/11/18		Battalion marched to TRAZEGNIES. Route HAUTE-FOLIE/ROEULX/LA LOUVIÈRE/LA HESTRE. Distance 16 miles. Good marching. No one fell out.	
	17/11/18		Battalion marched to CHARLEROI. Route SOUVRET/MONCEAU. Distance 7 miles.	
			Strength 36 Officers 858 O.R.	

WAR DIARY
or
INTELLIGENCE SUMMARY.
(Erase heading not required.)

Army Form C. 2118.

Place	Date	Hour	Summary of Events and Information	Remarks and references to Appendices
	18/12/18	—	Battalion marched to VITRIVAL. Route CHATELET/PRESLES. Distance 12 miles.	
	19/12/18	—	Battalion marched to WEPION via FOSSE. Distance 11 miles.	
WEPION	20/12/18		Arranging Billets etc.	
	21/12/18		Arranging Billets etc. 2/Lt Caldwell on leave to U.K.	
"	22/12/18		2/Lt. Low to U.K. conducting 38 miners for Demobilization. 2/Lt C. Hamilton to U.K. for Course. Divine Service.	
"	23/12/18		Battalion marched to AUVELAIS. Route SIX-BRAS/SART ST. LAURENT/FOSSE/FALISOLLE. Distance 15 miles. 2/Lt McBain & Cunningham to U.K. on leave.	
AUVELAIS	24/12/18		Arranging Billets. 2/Lt Sinclair to U.K. conducting miners for Demobilization. 2/Lt Lean appointed Bn. Educational Officer during absence of 2/Lt Sinclair.	
"	25/12/18		Christmas Day. Holiday.	
"	26/12/18		Coy. Parades and arranging Billets	
"	27/12/18		Arranging Billets and 30 yds range etc.	
"	28/12/18		Arranging Billets. Building Cookhouses Incinerator etc.	
"	29/12/18		Divine Service. Coy. Parades. Lt. Col Thirden appointed Brigade Musketry Officer.	
"	30/12/18		Arranging Billets.	
"	31/12/18		Holiday. Strength 31 Officers 788 O.R.	

A3 10245

WAR DIARY
or
INTELLIGENCE SUMMARY.
(Erase heading not required.)

Army Form C. 2118.

1/5 A&S.H.
Aug.
Vol. 10
12.M.

Place	Date	Hour	Summary of Events and Information	Remarks and references to Appendices
AUVELAIS	1/1/19	—	Holiday. — Strength 31 Offs. & 788 O.R. Maj J. Young M.C. awarded D.S.O. (Honorary Lt. Egypt)	
"	2/1/19	—	Batt. Route March. — To U.K.(leave):– Capt. & Adjt. J.M. Taylor M.C. & Revd Mr C. Belland C.F.	
"	3/1/19	—	C°Y Parades – To U.K.(leave) 2/Lt Carmichael.	
"	4/1/19	—	C°Y Parades.	
"	5/1/19	—	Divine Service – To A.D.M.S.(for temporary duty) Lt. W.A. Fraser M.C. – To U.K.(leave) 2/Lt W.S. Ritchie.	
"	6/1/19	—	C°Y Parades – To U.K.(Demobilisation) 13 O.R. & also 2 O.R. from L.T.M.B. 103 B^de – To U.K.(leave) Lt. G. Archer – D.U.K. M.S. Kenzie.	
"	7/1/19	—	From Hospital 2/Lt A. Moon. Batt. Drill.	
"	8/1/19	—	Lecture (L.O.) – Route March – To U.K.(leave & Hospital) 4 O.R.(regulars)	
"	9/1/19	—	Awarded Croix de Guerre (Belgian) C/Lt R. Kerr M.C. 2/Lt J.Y. Cunningham – N° 204 34 ¾ C.S.M. Drummond.(Ref Div. Order 8/1/19)	
"	10/1/19	—	Trooping Colours – From U.K.(leave) 2/Lt Caldwell – From Hospital Lt R.M. Dunn D.C.O. & 2/Lt H.M. Oliphant A.G.Y.	
"	11/1/19	—	To U.K.(Demobilisation) C/Lt Thomson – Lt Fleming M.C. – Lt Taunton – Lt Mc Kenzie – 2/Lt Scott – 2/Lt Bennie	
"	"	—	2/Lt Caldwell – 2/Lt J.B. Campbell. Also 4 O.R. – B^de Route March – 2/Lt Thom to Command C.E.Y.	
"	12/1/19	—	To U.K.(Demobilisation) 18 O.R. – To U.K.(leave) 2/Lt Mc Naughton, 2/Lt Mc Allan – Divine Service.	
"	13/1/19	—	C°Y Parades – To U.K.(Demobilisation) 9 O.R. – Lt N. McLeod (Lt. Adjt.) 2/Lts A.Y.S. H.) 4 Sergeants & Lt appointed B^de Education Officer 29/11/18	
"	14/1/19	—	Batt. Route March – To U.K.(Demobilisation) 30 O.R. – From U.K.(leave) 2/Lt M.S. Craig.	
"	15/1/19	—	Strength 23 Offs. & 680 O.R. Batt. Parade (Ceremonial) – To U.K.(Demobilisation) 4 2 O.R.	

Army Form C. 2118.

WAR DIARY
or
INTELLIGENCE SUMMARY.
(Erase heading not required.)

Place	Date	Hour	Summary of Events and Information	Remarks and references to Appendices
AUVELAIS	16/4/19	—	Inspection by G.O.C. Division of 103 B.gde.	
,,	17/4/19	—	C.O. Parades — Divisional Commander inspected Batt. Billets.	
,,	18/4/19	—	C.O. Parades — B.gde Boxing Comp. to Winners :- N°303149 P.C. McBride "B.Coy" (Runner-up Wright 27003 1/Lt Duncan "C.Coy")	
,,	19/4/19	—	Divine Service. (at 15.30 hours)	
,,	20/4/19	—	Batt. left AUVELAIS by train C.rest sent off by population, all ranks being very popular with the inhabitants & very kindly treated by them.	
En Route	,,	,,	7 O.R. (Leave) 2/Lt MAYNE N. McGlashan.	
,,	21/4/19	,,	Crossed Rhine & passing through Cologne and at SIEG-BURG station at 16.30 hours. Batt. detrained & took over Outpost positions from 24th Canadian Batt. Position of Companies as follows :- B.H.Q. (GEISTINGEN) "B.Coy" (at HENNEF) A. & C.Coy.an STIELDORF "C.Coy" (at ROTT & SOVEN) "D.Coy" (at DAMBROICH).	
GEISTINGEN	22/4/19	,,	Outpost Routine	
,,	23/4/19	,,	Outpost Routine	
,,	24/4/19	,,	Outpost Routine — Demobilly & exhibit on leave in U.K. 7 O.R. — Farm leave to U.K. Maj. J. Young D.S.O. M.C.)	
,,	,,	,,	2/Lt McKiernan & 2/Lt Ritchie.	
,,	25/4/19	,,	}	
,,	26/4/19	,,	} Outpost Routine	
,,	27/4/19	,,	}	

Army Form C. 2118.

WAR DIARY
or
INTELLIGENCE SUMMARY.
(Erase heading not required.)

Instructions regarding War Diaries and Intelligence Summaries are contained in F. S. Regs., Part II. and the Staff Manual respectively. Title pages will be prepared in manuscript.

Place	Date	Hour	Summary of Events and Information	Remarks and references to Appendices
GEISTINGEN	28/4/19	—	Outpost Routine – To Hospital Maj. J. Young, D.S.O. M.C., 2/Lt McCrae, 2/Lt R. McQuaile.	
"	29/4/19	—	Outpost Routine – Rev. Mr Lelland C.F. from leave to U.K.	
"	30/4/19	—	Outpost Routine – Honours & Awards No 200319 Sergt. D.T. Harrison, 200336 L/Cpl A. Goodall (Extract from Times 21-1-19 M.S. Medal)	
"	31/4/19	—	Outpost Routine.	

Archibald
Bunn Lt. Col.
Commdg. 1/5th R. Hldrs.

WAR DIARY (FEBRUARY) 1919
INTELLIGENCE SUMMARY

(1)

Instructions regarding War Diaries and Intelligence Summaries are contained in F.S. Regs., Part II. and the Staff Manual respectively. Title pages will be prepared in manuscript.

(Erase heading not required.)

Place	Date	Hour	Summary of Events and Information	Remarks and references to Appendices
GEISTINGEN	1-2-19		Outpost Routine.	
GEISTINGEN	2-2-19		Batt. relieved in Outpost Line by 1/5th Border Regt. "A", "B", "C" & "D" Coys & Bn. H.Q. moved to SIEG-BURG PRISON independently on relief being completed; Bn. 14 Q with "B" Coy arriving there at 16.15 hours.	
SIEG-BURG	"			
SIEG-BURG	3-2-19		Batt. marched to WAHN Barracks arriving about 14.00 hours. To U.K. (leave) 2/Lt C.W. Hobroyd.	
WAHN	"		To U.K.(sick) 2/Lt J. Main — Appt^d. Acting Adjt., 2/Lt W.S. Ritchie.	
WAHN	4-2-19		Coy Parades — Death (Influenza) No. 5564 Pte Counter R. H.Q. Coy.	
"	5-2-19		Coy Parades — Extension of leave (pending demobilization) to 2/Lt J. Carmichael to 3-2-19.	
	"		Lt. R. Austin appt^d. Acting Baptain (34th Div. Memo A.4/344 of 31-1-19).	
"	6-2-19		Coy Parades — To U.K. (demobilization) 14 O.R. — Extension of leave 2/Lt J.Y. Cunningham, to 23-1-19	
	"		on urgent private affairs (34th Div. A.2899)	
"	7-2-19		Coy Parades — To U.K. (demobilization) Lt T. Shearer & 4 O.R.	M^y
"	8-2-19		Batt. Route March — To U.K. (demobilization) 9 O.R.	
"	9-2-19		Divine Service — To U.K. (demobilization) 6 O.R. To U.K. (leave) 2/Lt J. Thom — To hospital 2/Lt F. Wilkinson M.M.	
"	9-2-19		From Hospital (Bonn) Maj. J. Young D.S.O. M.C. — To U.K. (sick) 2/Lt A.K. Quaile.	
"	10-2-19		Coy Parades — Lt W.A. Fraser M.C. relieved from special mission into Germany. (Prisoner of war search).	
"	11-2-19		Coy Parade — Inspection of Barracks by Divisional General.	
"	12-2-19		Batt. Parade — To U.K. (demobilization) 5 O.R. To U.K. (Regular) 16 O.R.	

(2)

Army Form C. 2118.

WAR DIARY (FEBRUARY 1919)
or
INTELLIGENCE SUMMARY.
(Erase heading not required.)

Instructions regarding War Diaries and Intelligence Summaries are contained in F.S. Regs., Part II. and the Staff Manual respectively. Title pages will be prepared in manuscript.

Place	Date	Hour	Summary of Events and Information	Remarks and references to Appendices
WAHN	13·2·19	----	Batt: Rate March – To U·K· (demobilization) 110 O·R· – 76th E·N·N·E·F·(at Station)7/Lt J.McNaughton as Interpreter.	
"	14·2·19	----	6·9 Parades – To U.K (demobilized) Rev R.S.McLelland (C.F.) + 13 O.R.	
"	15·2·19	----	Instructor of Bayonets – To U·K· (demobilized) 5 O·R·	
"	16·2·19		Divine Service – To U·K· (demobilized) 1/3 O·R·	
"	17·2·19 / 18·2·19		C9 Parades, Inspection & Presentation of Decorations by Divisional General. [To U·K· (demobilized) 1/Lt A.C. Kennedy.] Recipients :- Capt. R. Kerr M.C. (presented with Croix de Guerre (Belgium)) – C.S.M. Brunnemann (also with Croix de Guerre (Belgium))	
"	19·2·19		C9 Parades – Honours & Awards :- N9 4094 Sergt J. Lyons, Batn M.M. (Auth 34th Div. R.O. 64 of 14·2·19.	
"	" "		From U.K. (leave) Capt T.M.Taylor M.C. – From Hospital (Bonn) 7/Lt R. Wilkinson M.M.	
"	20·2·19		C9 Parades – To U·K· (demobilized) 1/2 O.R.	
"	21·2·19		C9 Parades Football :- Semi-final for Divisional & commandants Cup. Result 1/5 A.&S.H. 2 goals, 1/4 L&estins R.F. 1 goal (played SIEGBURG)	
"	22·2·19		To U.K.(demobilized) 6 O.R. – To 160 Bge R.F.A. (for attachment) Lt S. Park 4/Lt Thomson M.C., D.C.M. From U.K. (leave) 7/Lt Penicott.	
"	23·2·19		Divine Service – To U.K. (demobilized) 1/3 O.R.	
WAHN {HENNEF	24·2·19		Left WAHN (train) 0730 hours, Arrd HENNEF at 0815 hours. B.H.Q. at The Schloss (Allner) – "D" (advanced Cpy) at BROL.	
HENNEF	25·2·19		Outpost Routine. Divisional Cross Country Relay Race (One Mile) Team of 20. Result 1/5 A.&S.H. (1st) – Machine Gun Corps (2nd) 1/4 T. Gordon (2nd place) – 1/6 J.McTaggart M.C. (3rd place). Result counts towards Divisional Cob'n Cup.	
"	26·2·19		Running Teams :- Capt A.F.Y. J.M.Taylor, M.C. – 7/Lt Pa. Heinou – 7/Lt Wilkinson, M.M. – 7/Lt Oliphant. Pte H Hammond – Shevan – Irvine – white – 4/c Cairns – C.S.M. O'Connell – S.Sgt Lyon "Mob'd" Mc Criquet – Quigley – Tervin – McCafferty – Wallace – S.S.Kennedy.	
"	" "		Outpost Routine – Attached to Unit, Rev. R. Macdonald. (C.F.)	
"	27·2·19		Outpost Routine. Honours & Awards :- N9 200 31 S9L Brackenridge H. awarded the D.C.M. (Auth. London Gazette 1·1·19 N9 3109 ₤/3157 Sgt Hay H. C.E C.O.y. mentioned in Despatches 8·11·18 – Transferred To U.K. 15·2·19 – 7/Lt J.McBrae (31 days) Auth: 114/G.M. 103 Bde S.C.3/817	Silver Medals
"	28·2·19			

A.Wilson Lieut. Col.
Commd. 6th Bn. A.&S. Highr.

2353. Wt. W2514/1454 700,000 5/15 D.D. & L. A.D.S.S./Forms/C. 2118.

ORIGINAL.

SECRET.

WAR DIARY.
- OF -
1/5th ARGYLL & SUTHERLAND HIGHLANDERS.

1st March 1919 to 31st March 1919.

VOLUME 6

Lieut. Colonel,
Commanding 1/5th Bn. Argyll & Sutherland

1st High. Bde. 186 Inf. Bde.

Volume 6 Sheet 1. 1/5th A. & S.H.

Army Form C. 2118.

No. AT 16/452
D... 4/4/19.

WAR DIARY or INTELLIGENCE SUMMARY.
(Erase heading not required.)

Instructions regarding War Diaries and Intelligence Summaries are contained in F. S. Regs., Part II. and the Staff Manual respectively. Title pages will be prepared in manuscript.

Place	Date	Hour	Summary of Events and Information	Remarks and references to Appendices
HENNEF	1/3/19		Outpost Duty. A.B.+C Coys. at HENNEF. D Coy at BRÜH. Strength. 314 Officers 652 other ranks. 5th A.+S.H. now forms of Battalion Companies for Divisional Commands C/6. (5th A+S.H - 3 (5th Div.) Corps/ 3th A.M.S.C - 1	
HENNEF	2/3/19		Outpost Duty. Divine Service.	
HENNEF	3/3/19		Outpost Duty.	
HENNEF	4/3/19		Outpost Duty.	
HENNEF	5/3/19		Outpost Duty.	
HENNEF	6/3/19		Outpost Duty.	
HENNEF	7/3/19		Relieved by 10 W. Royal West Kent Regt. Bn. moved by train to HAHN. Barracks.	
WAHN	8/3/19		Battalion moved by rail to MECHERNICH AREA. Detrained at SATZVEG. Left. 103rd Regt 34th Division. Relieved 4/7nd R.S. Regt. Highland Division.	
ENZEN	9/3/19		Bn. HQ at ENZEN also D Coy. A + C Coys. at OBB-GARTZEN, B Coy at UEPERTCH.	
ENZEN	10/3/19		Company Parades. Advance party left for BLATZHEIM.	
ENZEN	11/3/19		Battalion marched to ZÜLPICH and entrained for BUIR. Bn. HQ at BERGERHAUSEN.	
BERGERHAUSEN	12/3/19		A.B.+C Coys at BLATZHEIM. D Coy at BÜHEM.	
"	13/3/19		Draft of 4 Officers and 143 other ranks joined from 6th A.+S.H.	
"	14/3/19		Company Parades and Recruitment Training. Con dim. Parades and Recruitment Training.	

Army Form C. 2118.

1/5" A. & S.H.

Volume 6 (Sect.) WAR DIARY
or
INTELLIGENCE SUMMARY.

(Erase heading not required.)

Instructions regarding War Diaries and Intelligence Summaries are contained in F. S. Regs. Part II. and the Staff Manual respectively. Title pages will be prepared in manuscript.

Place	Date	Hour	Summary of Events and Information	Remarks and references to Appendices
BERGEHAUSEN	15/3/19		Company Parade & Recruitmental Training. Strength 35 Officers 998 other ranks.	
"	16/3/19		Company Parade & Church Parade. Recruital Training	
"	17/3/19		Battalion Route March. Recruitmental Training.	
"	18/3/19		Company Parade & Specialists Classes. Recruitmental Training.	
"	19/3/19		Battalion Drill at BLATZHEIM. Recrutional Training.	
"	20/3/19		Battalion Route March. Route GOLZHEIM - ESCHWEILER - BOUHEIM - BLATZHEIM.	
"	21/3/19		Battalion Parade. Recrutional Training.	
"	22/3/19		Very Wet. Parades under Coy. Commanders. Capt A.H. Fyffe A.U.R. for demobilization	
"	23/3/19		Divine Service. Rev C.R. MacDonald C.F. good and wet.	
"	24/3/19		Battalion Parade & Recrutional Training.	
"	25/3/19		Company Parades & Recrutional Training.	
"	26/3/19		Battalion Parade & Recrutional Training.	
"	27/3/19		Route March. Route GOLZHEIM - BUIR - MANHEIM - BLATZHEIM. 5 Officers to 2nd A.I.S.H.	
"	28/3/19		Company Parades & Recrutional Training.	
"	29/3/19		Battalion Parade & Recrutional Training.	
"	30/3/19		Divine Service	
"	31/3/19		Company Parades & Recrutional Training. Strength 36 Officers 983 other ranks. A.J. Wilson Lieut Col. Comdg 1/5th Bn A.& S.H.

FOR OFFICIAL USE ONLY

TOURNAI 5

1/100,000

2/ Lunts

McCrae

BRUSSELS 6.

EDITION 2.
BELGIUM

Scale $\frac{1}{100,000}$.

4 MAESEYCK	7 LIÈGE	9 MARCHE	10 ARLON
3 ANTWERP	6 BRUSSELS	8 NAMUR	19 MÉZIÈRES
2 GHENT	5 TOURNAI	12 VALENCIENNES	18 ST QUENTIN
1A DUNKERQUE / OSTEND / 5A HAZEBROUCK	11 LENS	17 AMIENS	
13 CALAIS	14 ABBEVILLE		

BELGIUM 1:100,000

Geographical Section, General Staff. N° 2364.

→ = Route
◯ = Place Billeted

Townships
Hamlets
Canal or waterway
Chateau. Farm.
Church or Chapel
Fort
Frontier line
Heights in metres
Lighthouse
Orchard

BRUSSELS 6.

EDITION 2.
BELGIUM

Scale $\frac{1}{100,000}$.

4 MAESEYCK	7 LIEGE	9 MARCHE	10 ARLON
3 ANTWERP	6 BRUSSELS	8 NAMUR	19 MÉZIÈRES
2 GHENT	5 TOURNAI	12 VALENCIENNES	18 ST. QUENTIN
DUNKERQUE / 5A OSTEND	11 HAZEBROUCK / LENS	17 AMIENS	
13 CALAIS	14 ABBEVILLE		

WO 95 2466/2

5 BN KING'S OWN SCOTTISH BORDERERS

1918 APRIL – 1919 MARCH

155th Brigade.

52nd Division

Battalion disembarked MARSEILLES from EGYPT 17.4.18

1/5th BATTALION

KING'S OWN SCOTTISH BORDERERS

APRIL 1918.

SECRET 1 3rd Seldon
                  EEF

War Diary for the
month of April from
the unit under my
Command is sent herewith

                    McCray
                  Leafready
                   for OC
  45-k   ? ? ?

Army Form C. 2118.

WAR DIARY
or
INTELLIGENCE SUMMARY.

April 1915   Vol XXXVI

(Erase heading not required.)

Instructions regarding War Diaries and Intelligence Summaries are contained in F. S. Regs., Part II. and the Staff Manual respectively. Title pages will be prepared in manuscript.

Place	Date	Hour	Summary of Events and Information	Remarks and references to Appendices
SARONA	April 1915 1		Bn moved from SARONA at 1800 & marched to Divisional Camp at SURAFEND where Division was concentrating preparatory to embarkation to FRANCE. Arrived at 2230 & went into bivouac. Fine night.	
SURAFEND new LUDD	2		Men were very cheery & marched extra well. Fine night. Day spent in handing in stores surplus to Establishment B.E.F. FRANCE. This included 33 map perque L.S. & Bivouac Sheets Drew waterproof sheets for hospital 1 officer Reginald from hospital 12/APR/94 2 officers	2/Lt J. HOOD 2/Lt W. ROBINSON 2/Lt OWF RICHARDSON
	3		Handed in all transport lorries & animals. Bn passed through Gas Cloud.	
	4		Entrained at LUDD at 1800 for KANTARA on train of 37 trucks. 1 Officer 2 i/c Command left Bn to take new command 1/5 SUFFOLK REGIMENT	Major W.N. CAMPBELL
KANTARA	5		Arrived at KANTARA at 1000 & marched to 52nd Details Camp. Completed men with serge clothing. 2 officers joined Bn for duty. 75 OR. entrained for ALEXANDRIA at 2300 at KANTARA WEST 1 train 37 trucks 1 Officer & Cook Ammunition Sergeant	2/Lt G.W. JENKINS 2/Lt A.R. JOHNSTON A/Staff Sgt. HEATH AV.C.

Army Form C. 2118.

WAR DIARY
or
INTELLIGENCE SUMMARY.

Vol XXXVI

April 1918

(Erase heading not required.)

Instructions regarding War Diaries and Intelligence Summaries are contained in F.S. Regs., Part II. and the Staff Manual respectively. Title pages will be prepared in manuscript.

Place	Date 1918	Hour	Summary of Events and Information	Remarks and references to Appendices
ALEXANDRIA	6		Arrived at GABBARY DOCKS ALEXANDRIA at 10.00. Embarked on HMT KAISER-I-HIND PT.O. Steamship Company. All had embarked by 12.00. Other troops on board 1/4 R.S.F. & 1/5 A.P.S.H. 1 Section 3rd Welsh L.F.A. 155 Bde H.Q. Leave ashore to Officers only.	Major P.S.L. BEAVER Wiltshire Regiment in Command as Second in Command. 2/Lt H.M.T.BAYTA 2/Lt R.B. ORR 2/Lt H.A. SCOTT L/Sgt MORRISON Sgt AIRDRIE
	7		1 Officer joined.	
	8		nil	
	9		3 Officers proceeded to KANTARA for RFC 2 O.R.	
	10		Ship went into outer harbour at 16.00	
	11		Ship sailed at 14.00. Calm night	
	12		a little rough in forenoon	
	13		very cold day	
	14		Strong breeze but very slight motion. Church Parade.	

D. D. & L., London, E.C.
(8069) Wt W17771/M2053 750,000 5/17 Sch. 82 Forms/C2118/14

WAR DIARY
or
INTELLIGENCE SUMMARY.
(Erase heading not required.)

Army Form C. 2118.

VOL XXXVI
April 1918

Place	Date	Hour	Summary of Events and Information	Remarks and references to Appendices
H.M.T. KALBER-I-HIND	15	—	Calm day. Sports for men.	
	16	—	Calm day. Pillow alarm.	
MARSEILLES	17	—	Entered harbour of MARSEILLES at 0800. Tied up at quay 0800. Disembarked by 1330 being about an hour waiting for kit & rain. Coast first till 1500. Men entrained marching for 1 bunker. Marched up through town to MOSSO Camp at end of the CORNICHE a distance of over 5 miles. Men wear very tired. Rations issued to men at 1830. Men billeted in tents & huts. Tea issued to men at about 1900. Men about 10/11 per tent. Stores supplied 29. 3 rugs. Found no Said to be a certain ephemeris noted with 4 R.S.F. 150F 20 Britannia Major P.S.L.BEAVER. Officer temporarily attached. 1 officer confined to Camp. Officers up to 50% to take leave to MARSEILLES.	
MOSSO CAMP	18	—	Men confined to Camp.	
TRAIN	19	—	Left MOSSO CAMP at 0315 & marched to Railway Station at DOCKS (Point 1) arrived there 0630 & found station very congested, only 3 Coys Ends. for into it. A Train was unloading at the time.	

Army Form C. 2118.

WAR DIARY
or
INTELLIGENCE SUMMARY.
(Erase heading not required.)

Vol XXX VI
April 1915

Instructions regarding War Diaries and Intelligence Summaries are contained in F. S. Regs., Part II. and the Staff Manual respectively. Title pages will be prepared in manuscript.

Place	Date	Hour	Summary of Events and Information	Remarks and references to Appendices
TRAIN	April 19		Men issued with breakfast at station at 0800. Entrained at 0900. Train left at 0930. 37 men were in each truck, 8 & 6 at 3rd Class Carriage. Mostly wooden seats. Reached MIRAMAR at 1400 & issued tea to men.	
	20		Stopped at 0700 & issued rations to Companies. The issue from Coys to men was unsatisfactory as Carriages did not connect to Sen. Proceeded to C.O.M.S.s. Ends was up ready by Trains MIOMY Stopped at 0900 & issued tea to men for breakfast. JUVISSY between 0900 & 1000 (return) tea & rations to men	
	21		Stopped at & supplied A & (some) tea & rations to men.	
	22		Arrived at NOYELLES SUR MER at 0800. Marched to rest camp & obtained breakfast for men at 0900. At 1100 marched 6 miles to FOREST MONTIERS where the Bn went into billets. Men were accommodated in barns & sheds. Officers in houses with beds. The billets were in the whole good. No sanitary arrangements.	
FOREST MONTIERS				

Army Form C. 2118.

WAR DIARY
or
INTELLIGENCE SUMMARY.
(Erase heading not required.)

Vol XXXVI
April 1918

Place	Date	Hour	Summary of Events and Information	Remarks and references to Appendices
FORET MONTIERS	23		Settling down in billets & kit inspection. 1 Officer sent to 5th Romain Bn Royal Irish Rgt. as LG instructor	2/Lt R GILLESPIE
	24		Close order drill — Coys marched to RVF for hot spray baths 4 miles. 1 Warrant Officer joined as P.T. & Bayonet fighting Instructor	CSM GILPIN
	25		Coys marched to RVF (4 miles) for hot spray baths. Some flu still going. Bayonet fighting instruction 3½ NCOs & Men Musketry, 2 water courts, 1 Mystore 1 hrs Coys Zpunk Instruction with saddlery lecture m/Jas & Bayonet fighting	m/Sgt Claymore
	26		Route march of 9 miles in FORETT DE CRECY	
	27		Passed C in C F.M. Sir DOUGLAS HAIG who stopped his car & inspected the Bn as it marched past. He made favourable comments on the men's physique. Gen LAWRENCE was also present. late CommandR of the Division. Bayonet fighting Instructor left for another unit	CSM GILPIN
	28		Church Parade. Preparation for march to RVE & entrainment for AIRE on 29th. New clothing issued to large percentage of men. 8 pack animals & 1 Limbered & 1 G.S. limpets with 1 CQMS & 2 men per Coy sent on as Billeting Party	

Army Form C. 2118.

WAR DIARY
or
INTELLIGENCE SUMMARY.
(Erase heading not required.)

Vol XXVI April 1918

Place	Date	Hour	Summary of Events and Information	Remarks and references to Appendices
WITTE	April 29		Gunfire supplied to Bn at 0415. Bn left starting point ¾ mile NW of FORREST MONIERS at 0600 & marched to RUE JATON reaching there at 0710. Breakfast served to men at station. Troops & Platoon Kitchen was in filthy condition. horses & were in a filthy condition. Men & horses Aire at 1710. Marched to WITTE & were met by Lt RICHARDSON who had arranged billets satisfactorily. D Coy arrived at 2000. Billets were in fair condition.	
	30		100 men of "C" Coy arrived at 0800. Brewer occupied getting into billets. Afternoon men free.	

Richard N. Gordon Lt Col
Cmdg 1/5 R. Kent R. B.

May 1st 1918

1/5th K.O.S. Borderers

Appendix No 1 to War Diary for month of February, 1918.

		offrs	o.rs
(a)	Strength of Unit 31/3/18	35	805

(b). Casualties during month.

	offrs	o.rs
Killed	-	-
Wounded	-	1
Missing	-	-
Sick	1	26
	1	27

(c). Transferred etc.	5	4
(d). Reinforcements	5	96
(e). Strength of Unit 30/4/18	34	870

ATTACHED 52ND. DIVISION
155TH INFY BDE

34 DIV 102 BDE

1-5TH BN K. O. S. B.

APR - JUN 1918

ATTACHED 52ND. DIVISION
155TH INFY BDE

No 2

WAR DIARY
OF
1/5th King's Own Scottish Borderers.
1-5-18 — 31-5-18

VOL - xxxvii -

CONFIDENTIAL

9.W.
10 sheets

Army Form C. 2118.

WAR DIARY
or
INTELLIGENCE SUMMARY.

(Erase heading not required.)

Vol XXXVIII
May 1918

Place	Date	Hour	Summary of Events and Information	Remarks and references to Appendices
WITTE	May 1		1 Officer 3 s. O.R. attached to 413 Cny RE as pioneers Company Training 1 O/y S.M. arrived as transport fighting instructor	2/Lt. JNINSON CSM HEMMINGS Canadian Instr.
	2		Bn march to & from South of MAMETZ & passed through Gas Sheds many Box Respirators redamped – new giltes Bn's were taken & midday meal eaten at roadside. Passed WITTE at 15.30. 2nd Lieut R. been met Bn at entrance to village. Mens boots in bad condition. 1 Officer to hospital	
	3		20 O.R. attached to 15 st LTM Battery for duty. Coy training in morning. 23 Officers proceeded & took turns to lectures on recent operations Coy Officer C. in C. came to meeting & addressed & 1 Officer to hospital Bn Gas 1 N.C.O & 52 O.R. sent to MATRINGHEM	2/Lt. J.B. PRINGLE 2/Lt. J.B. PRINGLE Lieut Fleming
	4		div Coy training in forenoon. Details of Bn sent to MAMETZ for Gas Training	

Army Form C. 2118.

WAR DIARY
or
INTELLIGENCE SUMMARY.
(Erase heading not required.)

VOL XXXVI
May 1918

Place	Date	Hour	Summary of Events and Information	Remarks and references to Appendices
WITTES	5	—	Training	
	6	—	do	
NEUVILLE ST VAAST	7	—	Bn paraded at 0600 & marched to AIRE. Eventually arrived at MAROEUIL at 1700. Train 2 hours late. They were picked up with ta & RGC took Co.s in car to firing line. Bn reached HQ Camp at Maurille St Vaast at 2200.	
	8	—	Bn moved into line in Right Subsector of Division opposite ARLEUX. Took over from 2 Coys 1/7 GORDONS & 2 Coys 1/7 Black Watr. HQ Headquarters to a company headquarters there was no available to a company Hqrs & no buried cable & new wire system. There was no buried cable & new difficulty was experienced owing to this. The Bn HQ was too small to the present? was great.	
	9	—	Nil. Leave to UK. commenced 4 Officers & 85 per day. 1 Officer every 5 days	
	10	—	German prisoner taken at a bomb SAP. Gas projector attack we sent over 656 gas shells into ARLEUX	
	11	—	Strong line to Right	
	12	—	Quiet day. 1 Offr & 9 O.R to L.G. course Le TOUQUET	

Army Form C. 2118.

WAR DIARY
or
INTELLIGENCE SUMMARY.
(Erase heading not required.)

May 1915
Vol XXVII

Place	Date	Hour	Summary of Events and Information	Remarks and references to Appendices
SAILLY	May 13		Relieved 6th KOSB. 2 Coys inc in line & 2 in support. 520R from Argyle rejoined the Bn. Made matters much easier at the firing line. 1st Party of 1 Mr & 30 OR. went on leave to England. Hereafter average of 4 per day.	
	14		3 officers reported sick. 2Lt TRICOLL, JALSTON, & RJOHNSTON, 56 who has previously passed into ARLEUX on H.I.	
	15		Bn relieved by 156 Bde in line. The actual relief being the 1/9 Scottish Rifles. Daylight relief was attempted but the trenches were so difficult & by that relief was not completed till 2300.	
	16		Day of rest in billets & cleaning up.	
	17		Started programme of training.	
	18		Training to his battn.	
	19		Sunday Church Parade. L/Cpl Kirwin John Egypt Mo attached to 1/3 LFA	

WAR DIARY or INTELLIGENCE SUMMARY

Army Form C. 2118.

Vol XXVII May 1915.

Place	Date	Hour	Summary of Events and Information	Remarks and references to Appendices
MONT ST ELOY	May 20		3 Officers joined for duty. 2/LT D.MILLER KOSB LT M. CRICHTON H.L.I. } from U.K LT G.B.BARR H.L.I.	
	21		Co & Coy Cmdrs went on reconnaissance of new line. Germans sent 8 5.9 shells into our camp. St ELOY	
	22		2/Lt A KAYE 9/Lt R GILLESPIE } returned to hospital.	
	23		Co & Coy Commanders reconnoitred new position in line. nil.	
VIMY TRENCHES	24		Battalion relieved 1/5 H.L.I. in ARLEUX Battalion subsector in 3rd & 4th lines. Bn HQ in VIMY. Relief completed at 24.30. 25th 3/Seaforths Bde Coy. 4th line "D" Coy. A Coy in Bn Reserve. Fine day.	
	25		Area shelled but not at all severely mostly 4.2". Day fine & trenches drying up again.	

Army Form C. 2118.

WAR DIARY
or
INTELLIGENCE SUMMARY.
(Erase heading not required.)

May 1915
Vol. XXXVII.

Instructions regarding War Diaries and Intelligence Summaries are contained in F. S. Regs., Part II. and the Staff Manual respectively. Title pages will be prepared in manuscript.

Place	Date	Hour	Summary of Events and Information	Remarks and references to Appendices
VIMY	26		A quiet day.	
Trsas E	27		At 0100 The enemy commenced a bombardment with gas shells of the VIMY town area. Till 0230 he employed a fairly rapid rapid fire from guns of light calibre, probably 7.7cm. From 0230 till 0430 this was the of fire and used slower. Scattered the number of shells a follows:	
May 26			90 mins at 10 rounds per minute = 900	
			120 mins at 5 rounds per minute = 600	1500 shells
			The gas was almost entirely yellow cross (mustard). A few shells of heavy calibre probably 8" came over. These were heard with a very slight report & a peculiar smell of garlic. Small of garlic (Allegars) was noted. The wind was from the N.W. + a light breeze. All made every preparation at once & put on their masks. The heavie enemy attacked the town from one + practised L-BROWN TRENCH on the back of the town. At 0500 the O.C. Quoin inspected his dugouts + returned for breakfast. The other tr billets were also considered safe as there was practically no smell of gas. At 0900 3 stretcher repras sick + were immediately evacuated to hospital. At 1100 a number of men reported sick + the number was increased during during the day. After our Adren at 0500 + evidently reported this & became & whole dug out full of men were of stretcher. The latest proved	

WAR DIARY
or
INTELLIGENCE SUMMARY.
(Erase heading not required.)

Army Form C. 2118.

May 1915
Vol XXVII

Place	Date	Hour	Summary of Events and Information	Remarks and references to Appendices
MAY T28a c. 6	May 27		up to this evening was 36 to hospital & 4 under observation. During the day many men were placed through sitting in the open near where shells had fallen. Because of the rough nature of the ground, large shell holes, broken masonry & long grass the gas shell holes could not as a rule be found. It seems certain he obtained. It is evident that when an area has been shelled with yellow cross, it must be evacuated or the men must wear gas helmets the whole time they occupy it. The smell is so faint that it is impossible to say who has an area is free or not. Two men suffered from eye trouble through sitting in a latrine seat over which some of the liquid must have been sprayed. No one experienced any smarting sensation in the eyes or nose at first. These develope later. The men badly gassed so vomited some 8 hours or so later. The nurses cases were those who had taken exercise after being in the gas. The day was quiet & only a few shells were put over during the night. Signed: (illegible) Lieut. Signed 2nd Lieut. G.H. JENKINS took over Bn. Signals when 2/Lt. LITTLE returned to his Bn	

WAR DIARY or INTELLIGENCE SUMMARY

Army Form C. 2118.

WO/XX/V/1
May 1918

Place	Date	Hour	Summary of Events and Information	Remarks and references to Appendices
VIMY 7.20.C.2.1	May 28		In the morning several more cases of gas (mustard) & there was still a smell of gas sufficiently irritant to move battalion Headquarters to D. Coy HQ as there was no space available elsewhere. This HQ was very inconvenient but there was no where else to go. The H.Q & what was left of "C" Coy (Mr Whitley) moved to the new dugouts in 2.5 & 3.5 along the NEW BRUNSWICK ROAD. Aguirre Coy sat along the Divisional Front. Coy Casualties are 4 O.R. Two Officers, Whitley & Prust	
	29		Between 0200 & 0400 the enemy heavily shelled support lines & the forward Trenches nr. Stables & 2 supports to the Brigade. Little damage was done to trenches. The enemy shells VIMY from own heavy by where they with 5.9 H.E. till 2100. One of "A" Coy were injured. A quiet day otherwise weather finer since 25th May.	
	30		A quiet day. Glorious weather.	

WAR DIARY
or
INTELLIGENCE SUMMARY.

(Erase heading not required.)

Army Form C. 2118.

May 1918
XXXVII

Place	Date	Hour	Summary of Events and Information	Remarks and references to Appendices
VIMY T.20.c.2.1	1918 May 31	P.M.	During the evening the enemy sent over a number of 5"ish shells, which fell beside Headquarters but did no damage. A quiet day with a warm sun.	
			Richard N. Curtois Lt Col Cmdg 1/s. R of S 73	
			May 31st 1918	
			Casualties affecting battalion during May	Appendix I

5th S.A.I. Boedeker

Appendix No. 1 to War Diary for month of May 1918

(a) Strength of Unit 30/4/18.   Offrs 32   O.Rs 881

(b) Casualties during month -
　　Killed   -   1
　　Wounded   -   3
　　Missing   -   -
　　Sick   3   128
　　　　　　　 3   132

(c) Transferred etc   -   -

(d) Reinforcements   8   82

(e) Strength of Unit 31/5/18   37 - 831

CONFIDENTIAL 34

1/1 Vol 3

WAR DIARY

of

1/5th KING'S OWN SCOTTISH BORDERERS.

1-6-1918 — 30-6-1918.

VoL XXVIII

10.W.
11 whales

WAR DIARY or INTELLIGENCE SUMMARY

Army Form C. 2118.

Vol XXXVIII   **June 1916**

Place	Date	Hour	Summary of Events and Information	Remarks and references to Appendices
VIMY T/8.c.9.3	May 31st		Major the Officer reported for duty as 2nd in Command. Major R.R. BEAVER	
	June 1		Quiet day.	
	2		Relieved 7/5th R.S.F. in Right Front Sector of the Brigade in the TOAST SECTOR. Relief commenced at 9 am. "D" Coy. moving up the GRAND TRUNK TRENCH. "C" Coy. GERTIE TRENCH. "B" Coy. followed up GRAND TRUNK at 11 am. Headquarters moved at 2 pm. All Companies moved by sections at 5 minute interval. Relief with the exception of the Lewis posts in front was completed by 5 pm. The 6 lys. being in the from "S.B.6" from Right to left with "A" Coy in Support. The final relief was at 12.30 am on 3rd June. The day was Staff & no Enemy Baloons were up. At 9.30 pm the Enemy sent over about 20 casualties. 40 Blue Cross shells which burst with an HE explosion. Several men were slightly gassed but none sent to hospital	
	3		A Quiet day. Two O.R. awarded D.C.M. for pulling shells out of a burning Dump 240 200 Sergt. D CLARK 30576 S/Sgt. T. GAFFEY	
	4		A quiet day. Mlg Offr. Vaule proceeded to England for a Commission. Sgt. ORDYKES	

Army Form C. 2118.

WAR DIARY
or
INTELLIGENCE SUMMARY.
(Erase heading not required.)

June 1918.

Instructions regarding War Diaries and Intelligence Summaries are contained in F. S. Regs., Part II. and the Staff Manual respectively. Title pages will be prepared in manuscript.

Place	Date	Hour	Summary of Events and Information	Remarks and references to Appendices
Vimy	June 5	—	Quiet. Sniper firing from T100 on T9.6. no casualties	
	6	—	Enemy shelled our Strokes at intervals with H.E. & Shrapnel. Gas shells (yellow X) on T16. no casualties. Col. Toulson proceeded on leave to England. Major Beaver commanding Battn.	
	7	—	Very quiet.	
	8	—	Considerable amount of gas shelling (yellow X).	
	9	—	Shelled occasionally with H.E.	
	10	—	T16a + c shelled at intervals during day with 5.9 H.E. 2/Lt. Little to hospital.	
	11	—	Battn. relieved by 1/4th Sco. Rifles during day. Relief completed by 15.30. Moved down by sections along grande Trunk to Canada — along Canada to Peggie — down Peggie to embark, went and into Brown line. Left Brown line at S.246.71 and moved along Red tail duckboard to Humber Trench thence to La Folie Farm. Got 'buses from there to Mont St Eloy (Ottawa Camp FSd0S25)	
	12		Capt. Gilmour proceeded to England on leave. Capt. McGeorge to hospital.	
Mont St Eloy	13		Evidence of influenza throughout Battn.	

Army Form C. 2118.

WAR DIARY
or
INTELLIGENCE SUMMARY.
(Erase heading not required.)

June 1918

Place	Date	Hour	Summary of Events and Information	Remarks and references to Appendices
Mont St Eloy	14		Major O.S.L. Beaver & 2/Lt. Kay proceeded to hospital.	
	15		2/Lt. Hood proceeded to hospital. Enemy shelled vicinity of camp with H.V. high explosive. 3 rounds. Injury sustained by Lt. BARR, S.H.L.I. to hospital. Draft of 23 O.R. from the U.K.	
	16		2/Lt DUNN proceeded on leave to U.K. Two H.V. shells in vicinity of camp. 23.10 A third H.V. shell hit end of "B" boy but killing 3 men and wounding 10. 2/Lt. W.N. Robertson to Southern Training Centre (M.G.C.)	
	18		Draft of 28 O.R. from U.K.	
	19		Cpl. J.K. Hopkins to hospital. Infantry gallerie started. 84 O.R. to hospital	
THELUS CAVES	20		Battalion relieved 7th H.L.I. in reserve. Coys. & H.Q. in THELUS CAVES. Relief complete by 3 p.m. Lieut Shaw Rt. H.Q. in THELUS CAVES. R. cas. at 2/Lieut L. McDonald (3rd KORR's) & 2/Lieut A.B. Johnston to hospital	
	21	55	Lieuts R. Gillespie & Knowles, R. Johnston attend Tank demonstration at WAVRANS. all quiet. hive v story from h. ac	
	22			

Army Form C. 2118.

WAR DIARY
or
INTELLIGENCE SUMMARY.

Vol XXXVIII June 1915

(Erase heading not required.)

Place	Date	Hour	Summary of Events and Information	Remarks and references to Appendices
THBUS CAMPS A,B,C,D,F.	June 22		Strong wind from West. Quiet day.	
	23		Quiet day. 2/Lt R.N. Coulson returned from leave & resumed command.	
	24		Quiet day. Drafts from UK arrived for Bn from HH. 23 O.R. Hospital returned to duty 24 O.R. Hospital returned to duty 22 O.R.	
	25		Quiet day. Major A.L. CRAWFURD Gordon Highlanders returned 2/Lt H.H.A.21 for duty.	
	26		Quiet day.	
	27		Bn. moved to LE PENDU Camp ST ELOY commencing at 0700. Our was not relieved. This move was necessitated by an order for 3 Bns of the 52nd Division to move by bus to reform the 103rd Brigade of the 34th Division. The remaining 3 Bns Rec'd the same amount of leave as the former 4 Bns. The new brigade consists of 1/5-KOSB. 1/8 Sco. Rif. 1/5-A & S.H. Inspection of Bn by Genl Sir Aylmer Hunter-Weston, of 6 a.m. He has commanded the 8th Corps in GALLIPOLI. 1 Officer reported to 1st LFA Capt A.G.J. HUNTER RAMC, M.C., as Bn MO. Lt. P.G.J. O'FARRELL RAMC. 1 Officer reported for duty as Bn MO. Lt. P.G.J. O'FARRELL RAMC. Returned to duty from 155 Brig Pioneer Coy 2/Lt SCOTT Draft of 40 OR from 7/8 KOSB. 2/Lt ROBINSON	

Army Form C. 2118.

WAR DIARY
or
INTELLIGENCE SUMMARY.
(Erase heading not required.)

Vol XXVIII June 1915

Place	Date	Hour	Summary of Events and Information	Remarks and references to Appendices
OOST-CAPEL	June 28/15		Bn Entrained at 10.30 a.m. for BAMBECQUE along with 2nd SR & 5th A & SH. Started at 11.00 proceeding through AIRE, ST. OMER to ST MOMELIN arrived at BAMBECQUE at 22.30. From here a march was made of 3 miles to OOST CAPEL where billets of sorts were found. Bn. arrived for the night at 02.00. Draft of 39 o.R. from UK	
	29		Settling down in OOST-CAPEL. Bn now in 152nd Brigade Brig. Gen. CHAPUN from 1st CAMERONIANS 34th Division Maj. Gen. NICHOLSON 2nd Corps Lt. Gen. JACOB. 2nd Army Gen. PLUMER. Some Bombs flying the village at night. Draft received of 18 oR from UK RSF a hanging thigh.	
ST JANSTER BIEZEN	30		Marched in afternoon to ST. JANSTER BIEZEN where the Bn went into Camp in Huts. Some Shells fell in vicinity.	

Bn Strength return .... Appendix 1
Letter from G.O.C. .... Appendix 2
" Punjab Assn Appendix 3
1/5-Kings B. Speech from Corp.& Appendix 4

Richard N. Carton Lt Col
Cmdg 1/5-Kings B.

To:
   Lieut-Colonel R.N. COULSON, the Officers, Warrant Officers, Non-Commissioned Officers and Men of The King's Own Scottish Borderers.

It is with the greatest regret that I have to write you this farewell order.

Though I have only been associated with you, as your Divisional Commander, for the past 10 months, I have had ample time to judge of your splendid behaviour both in billets and in the Field.

From November 7th till December 23rd, 1917, you were called upon almost every day to take part in some offensive operation against the Turk and on every occasion you shewed the magnificent fighting quality you possessed.

You are now going to another Division and so are lost to the 52nd (Lowland) Division, but I can assure you that I and all the officers and men of the Lowland Division will watch your further movements with the greatest confidence and interest.

You and the other two Battalions leaving this Division will probably be formed into a Brigade. I want you never to forget that you once belonged to the 52nd Lowland Division.

Good-bye and the very best of good luck is the wish of your very grateful Divisional Commander.

26th June, 1918.

Major-General,
Commanding 52nd (Lowland) Division.

France.

Dear Colonel Coulson,

    In the absence of the Brigadier, it devolves on me to express the deep feeling of regret on the part of the Brigade at the departure of the 1/5th K.O.S.B. from the Division.

    For ten years we have been assosciated together in peace and war, at home and abroad, and we shall feel your departure very acutely.

    We feel sure that the spirit which has always animated the 155th Brigade and 52nd Lowland Division will continue to be exemplified by your Battalion in the new Division to which you have been transferred.

    All ranks wish you the best of luck, and look forward to a happy and speedy reunion at a not far distant date.

27th June, 1918.   Lieut.-Colonel,
                                         Comdg. 155th. Inf. Brigade.

Sir Aylmer Hunter-Weston, your Corps Commander in Gallipoli, has come here this afternoon to greet you, and to tell you how sorry he is that the exigencies of the military situation necessitate your leaving his command.

He has so bad a sore throat that he cannot speak to you himself, and he therefore desires me to speak for him.

This battalion did splendid service under Sir Aylmer Hunter-Weston on the Gallipoli Peninsula, and he has heard with pleasure of the fine service that you have rendered to the State in the heavy fighting in Egypt and Palestine. He knows that wherever you go, each individual in the Battalion will do his best, both by his conduct in billets and by his bravery in battle, to maintain the high reputation that previous members of the Battalion have made for it.

Sorry though you must be to temporarily sever your connection with the Lowland Division, the Corps Commander is glad to be able to tell you that you are going to a Division that is commanded by an old friend of his, General Nicholson, who was a Brigadier in the 29th Division alongside you on the Gallipoli Peninsula. You will, therefore, be going under a General alongside whom you have served in trying times, and in whom you will rightly have every confidence.

As his comrades in Gallipoli, and as brother Scots, Sir Aylmer Hunter-Weston gives you his heartiest greetings and good wishes. He will ever watch the career and doings of the Battalion and follow it with interest and good wishes. He wishes you good luck and goodbye, and hopes that you will soon come under his command again.

VOL XXXVIII
Appendix 4

1/5th K.O.S. Borderers —
Appendix No.1 — to War
Diary for Month of June
1918.

	Off	O.R's
(a) Strength of unit 31/5/18	39	831

(b) Casualties during
  month —
    Killed — 3
    Wounded — 14
    Missing — 1
    Sick 9 206
(c) Transferred etc — —

(d) Reinforcements 2 + 218

(e) Strength of unit 30/6/18 — 39 — 836
       & Int Struck off 85

34TH DIVISION
103RD INFY BDE

1-5TH K. O. S. BDRS.

~~JLY — DEC 1918~~
1918 APL — 1919 MAR

FROM EGYPT 52 DIV 155 BDE

TO LOWLAND BDE.
9 DIV

WAR DIARY

of

1/5th KING'S OWN SCOTTISH BORDERERS

From 1.7.1918. To. 31.7.1918.

Vol. XXXIX

WAR DIARY
INTELLIGENCE SUMMARY

Army Form C. 2118.
Vol. XXXIX
July 1915

Place	Date	Hour	Summary of Events and Information	Remarks and references to Appendices
ST JANSTER BEZEN	July 1 1915		Bn inspected in marching order by Maj Gen HETBY G.O.C. CHAPLIN. Men had not been able to wash. Equipment.	
	2		Bn inspected in marching order by Lt Gen JACOB, The Corps Commander. Men had washed equipment.	
	3		Bn inspected in marching order by Gen PLUMER The Army Commander.	
	4		10 Other ranks to hospital. Lt J.L.GRAY Recovered. East POPERINGHE reserve line with Tg Amn. Company training & musketry on 30 yds range.	
	5		1 Officer joins for duty. Asn Capt & Q.M. W.B.CHURCHILL Welsh Regt. Coy training & musketry on 30 yds range. 2nd Lt. W.G.LANGHAM H.Q. St OMER	
	6		Company training & musketry on 30yd range. 1 Officer joins for duty.	
	7		Bn. marches to PROVEN where battalion entrained for transport moved by march route. Arrives at 1730.	
CORNETTE D.35.d.3.4.	8		1 draft of 43 men joins battalion at PROVEN station. Other ranks very tidy & Bn reproduces into marching order. Commenced musketry on range at 0500. Musketry on duty at 0400. 4 hour musketry & other 2 hour drill. Bn. drill & rejoices much steady drill.	

Army Form C. 2118.

WAR DIARY
or
INTELLIGENCE SUMMARY.
(Erase heading not required.)

Vol XXXIX July, 1918

Place	Date	Hour	Summary of Events and Information	Remarks and references to Appendices
CORMETTE (1,2,3,&4)	9	—	Draft of 52 O.R. rejoined from hospital, same pto. Musketry on range 4 hrs Full 2 hrs. (½ hr stat'y 1½ hrs Art'llery preparation)	
	10	—	Musketry as above & Bn Drill Heavy rain in afternoon ruining Draft 9 O.R. ← 20 R from hospital. (2 Russians unable to speak English)	
	11	—	Musketry as above & 2 hrs training	
	12	—	Musketry as above including Platoon attack Competition. 5 Officers rejoined Bn from U.K. 2/Lt BLYTHE RHJ	
	13th	—	marched to ST OMER at 0730 & entrained for PROVEN	
PROVEN F.1, 2, 3, 5 Hut 29	14	—	Detraining at 1500 & occupied 3 camps adjoining Troops of 72 O.R. joined from UK. A very fine draft Sunday. Church parade & cleaning up. Coy Commanders reconnoitred BRAND HOECK LINE	
	15	—	Company training A & B Coys bathed M. FONQUERNE joined for duty as in Reg'tlers	
	16	—	Bn entrained at WAVENBURG. (H.Q. & B Coy (batt'n)) Statistical trains with Transport 4 days rations were carried. "C" Coy. marched to station & arrived there at 6pm. It was hoped they some of the rolling stock had been provided & there	

WAR DIARY
INTELLIGENCE SUMMARY

Army Form C. 2118.

Vol XXXIX   July 1918

Place	Date	Hour	Summary of Events and Information	Remarks and references to Appendices
PROYEN Sheet 27 F.1.d.2.5	16		Company which was in the same train as 103 Bde. HQ did not move till about 2 am.	Major B.M.M.D. LTOFMELL proceeded to join on appointment. Capt. J.F. MACLAY joined for duty as M.O.
	17.		The Bn, which was entrained at 10 pm was kept there till 11 pm, when it marched to the station arriving there at midnight. The men lay down on the platform & adjacent lines. At 2 am the train came in & the transport was loaded, men moved in by 3.30 & the Bn. less C. Coy entrained. The train moved out at 04.15.	
CHAMANT	18		At 10 am the train arrived at SENLIS & the Bn. detrained & proceeded as soon as the Bn. marched to CHAMANT & went into very comfortable billets. Ie. the French army & trench army. The division was not attacked.	
	19.		At 04.30 a telephone message & a warning order were received from Brigade ordering the Bn. to entrain at 07.00 in marching order carrying Lewis Guns & finance by hand. The Bn. was entrained by 07.30 & moved to a point between VAUMOISE & VAUCIENNES (SOISSONS VONVERS A.4.2.9.) Here it lay from & has a midday meal marching at 14.30 to billets at PEIGNEUX (BEAUVAIS L.3.2.2.) This was reached at 18.00 after a very fatiguing march.	

WAR DIARY
or
INTELLIGENCE SUMMARY.

(Erase heading not required.)

Army Form C. 2118.

VOL XXXIX   July 1918

Place	Date	Hour	Summary of Events and Information	Remarks and references to Appendices
FEIGNEUX (Bouais 1.3.2.2.)	1918 July 19		The men were much distressed with the full marching order & carrying 220 rounds of ammunition & in addition heavy guns & big pass. The Transport which had moved by a big road SENLIS – BARON – NANTEUIL – CREPY did not arrive till 2.30 at earliest 25 miles. An overnight meal was prepared by 2000.	
FEIGNEUX	20		Day spent in cleaning up. Bn moved to parade at 8.30 for parade dismissed & returned for 11.45. Heavy rain fell but most of men found shelter in buildings.	
SOUCY	21		Marched all night on very heavy roads 16 miles to SOUCY. Men were wearing fighting order with greatcoats & bandoliers round haversacks for the first time. The march was one of the worst trying we ever had. A great many men fell out, entirely from the new straps, but all the fifteen eventually they 8 or 9 am March discipline was very poor & must be improved. Bn bivouaced in the wood.	
	22		C.O. & 3 Coy Commanders with the interpreter went on to MONTREMBOEUF FARM near PERCY TIGNY & HENRIETTY FONT. Brigade orders to be in Divisional Reserve, the other two Brigades were to relieve the French in the line & attack. Bn marched at 8 am reached CHAVIGNY FARM at 15.30 in fighting order, moved on 10 pm through LONGPOINT & reached CAVE near MILLERS HELON at 01.30. Men slept in mapel woods. March discipline good	

D. D. & L., London, E.C. A905 Wt. V 171/M2031 750,000 5/17 Sch. 52 Forms C2118/14

WAR DIARY or INTELLIGENCE SUMMARY

Army Form C. 2118.

Vol XXIX
July 1918

Place	Date	Hour	Summary of Events and Information	Remarks and references to Appendices
MUNTRAM REDOUBT	July 23		Division ordered to attack in front from TRIM to COUTREMAIN. 101 & 102 Bdes in line 103 in Div Reserve. 10/K.O.S.B. & K.O.S.B. & Somerset Light Infantry in left Reserve. Bn moved at 0640 in fighting order carrying all bombs S.A.A. flares Verey Gun Magazines & Wirecutters. In woods at Arm Rd 71.42 at 1000 to await orders. Water was plentiful but no fires could be lit by day. Cookers arrived with a hot meal in the evening. Intermittent shelling all day.	
MUNTRAMBOEUF	24	do	Heavy shelling at 2am. 1 O.R. killed & 5 wounded by 101/102 Bde wire was not great success. Casualties about 33 officers & 650 OR. Lt GILLESPIE acted as Adjutant. Kitchen arrived. Evening Appr & Adjt T.D. CRAIG wounded. Bn Shellis intermittently attack.	
	25	do	Bn intermittently shelled 2 men gassed 3 or wounded S.A.A. y Bombs & Verey flares to 16 Devons from Trenches & S.A.A.	
	26	do	A showery day. Men resting & cleaning up. Intermittent shelling. 1 man wounded.	

WAR DIARY or INTELLIGENCE SUMMARY

Army Form C. 2118.

July 1918

Place	Date	Hour	Summary of Events and Information	Remarks and references to Appendices
BOIS DE BOEUF	July 1918 27		Moved to BOIS DU BOEUF at 2.00 arrived at 23.45. The Batt[n] arrived to find a large number of French in occupation of the Battalion area. Cooks and Transport arrived at 01.00 and the men got a hot meal. Cold night without cover in the wood. C.O. sent for by R.S.C. at 9 am & received instructions to reconnoitre for an attack on BEUGNEUX. The R.S.C. informed C.O. that the French had captured the BUTTÉ de CHALMONT and that an attack was to take place next morning instead of in two days time. C.O. and Lieut Crichton walked at 8 a.m. to BOIS de BAILLETTE & OUCHY la VILLE and reconnoitred towards BEUGNEUX – The latter village could not be seen as the shelling French line on the high ground screened the view	
	28			

WAR DIARY
INTELLIGENCE SUMMARY

XXXIX July 19-8

Place	Date	Hour	Summary of Events and Information	Remarks and references to Appendices
Bois du Boeuf	July 19/28		Capt Turner & Lieut Weir reconnoitred the ground in the afternoon. At 17.00 C.O. attended conference T.B.G. C.O.'s + CO's under Divisional Comd. & Bde after received verbal orders from D.S.C. There verbal orders communicated at 18.00 to Batt's Officers. The Batt's + 1st Cant Transport moved in Brigade by Guémy to Pier. Have Su Guides on track on French funct. The Batt's was heavily shelled leaving Bois du Bois 6775 and suffered a good many casualties, the leading Coy became scattered in the wood. The Batt's was halted on clearing the wood & runners & guides were sent back to find the rest of the Batt's. These returned having failed to find the Batt's and the C.O. decided to return him	After an 89 & his Comd to attack. Appen Nos 202 103-Suf. Appx 0. No 226
		20.45		

WAR DIARY or INTELLIGENCE SUMMARY

Army Form C. 2118.

July 1918

Place	Date	Hour	Summary of Events and Information	Remarks and references to Appendices
Bois de Reincourt	July 28		guide who stated that the other Coys and transport must have gone in all three guides in a different way. He and the half Coy moved up to first behind the new French line but no "Balls" could be found. He ascending 3	
dulls	29th		mmd had to come onto at 24.28. I was now 0300 and gave him his 0510. 6 dums were received to front the P.+S.H. to get the to take the S.R. O.S.D. line on the Edge of the line. Just then however the rest of the Coy mmd and 15th Div transport arrived at the Crossroads. The 15th Div transport had had a most difficult time under shell fire, but 6 gunse unit on the latter the transport. Bees Sergt S... was very sl...	

WAR DIARY or INTELLIGENCE SUMMARY

Army Form C. 2118.

XXXIX July 19-8

Place	Date	Hour	Summary of Events and Information	Remarks and references to Appendices
	July 29th		The Batt'n were relieved by 9/11 Together behind & later on barrage opened. On the heavy the reserve coy were on behind the other 3 coys. H.Q. was moved to Brigade advanced Report Centre at pt 116 at 32.91. The orders were received from coys that 07.00 was the zero hour all trailed out. The Batt'n fought its way through the woods to the S.W. of Beugneux & D coy reached the N.W. of the village & A part of the S.W. on the N scale, got to about 55.98. They hung on to & had all almost 800 who by then's called out withdraw to the and running. Started from the cross roads at 55.96. here they met hostile then other to M.G. fire from the N.E of area of the village.	

Army Form C. 2118.

WAR DIARY
or
INTELLIGENCE SUMMARY.
(Erase heading not required.)

XXXX
July 19-5

Place	Date	Hour	Summary of Events and Information	Remarks and references to Appendices
BOIS DE RAINETTE	July 29	6	The Loyal North Lancs came up from the S. at and French had started along thro' [Bois?]. 2 Coys A Coy were holding a line facing the village about through the D in BAISIEUX and the two black huts B & C Coys were at the S. end of the wood running S. W. from the D in BAISIEUX, at about 1300 a heavy barrage was put down & the French & especially came out behind our own but the Loyal North Lancs on our left were unable to hold on any longer & gave an order to Lieut. Richardson to fall back on the old [Roma?] defences. The 4 Coys re-organised. The Battalion casualties during the [?] were heavy.	

WAR DIARY
or
INTELLIGENCE SUMMARY.
(Erase heading not required.)

Army Form C. 2118.

Vol XXXIX
July 1918

Place	Date	Hour	Summary of Events and Information	Remarks and references to Appendices
BOIS DE BAILLEULE	July 29 1918		At first only 220 men could be accounted for but eventually men came back from other units & the strength rose to 530. The Bn received orders were received about noon to resume the attack on BEUGNEUX at 2.30 pm together with the Brigade. [B.M. 176]	Appendix III.
			This order was eventually cancelled & orders were issued for the Bn to occupy the Brigade frontage in the Old Paris Defences & for the J.F. & 9th & the 8th S.R. to push forward after dark as far as the line running OK & NW through the Black Huts & with other intermediate lines in support. This they succeeded in doing. There was heavy shelling throughout the night, but not many casualties in the Battalion.	

WAR DIARY
or
INTELLIGENCE SUMMARY.
(Erase heading not required.)

Army Form C. 2118.

Vol XXIX
July 1915

Place	Date	Hour	Summary of Events and Information	Remarks and references to Appendices
BOIS DE BAILLETTE	1/9 July 30		The Bn improved the old Paris Defences Line & dug a new trench for the Support Company. In the line from Right to Left were A & C & B Coy's with D Coy in Support. Heavy shelling at night.	
	31st		Day spent in improving the line. Written note issued for the second attack at BEUGNEUX 103 Bde N/w N° 226.	Appendix 4
			Coy Commanders at a conference at Bn HQ. at 4pm. when whole attack fire through & diagram of forming up places issued.	Diagram Appendix 5
			At 21.30 Coys moved out to position of assembly in front of Old Paris Defences. B&C in front line, A&D in second line. Coy's had each only 2 Platoons & these were no behind the other. Each Platoon had its Sections in second formation. Intervals 50 yds. Distances 150 yds.	

WAR DIARY
or
INTELLIGENCE SUMMARY.
(Erase heading not required.)

Army Form C. 2118.

XXXIX July 1918

Place	Date	Hour	Summary of Events and Information	Remarks and references to Appendices
REVSNEUX	July 31		This was not the case for now three minutes it was extremely difficult to find the Coys in the area & the dark. Eventually however each Coy & Coy was led up to the railway embankment & dug in. Coys were each in two lines in the order from right to left D. C. B. A Coys support in the rear B & D Coys at a distance of about 200 yds. H.Q. Coy was in a slg to & any of the coy about 200 yds in rear of A Coy. It was discovered later that - about 100 yards to the right flank of the Coy dug line there was an Enemy trench which enfiladed our line	

WAR DIARY
or
INTELLIGENCE SUMMARY.
(Erase heading not required.)

Army Form C. 2118.

VOL XXXIX July 1915

Place	Date	Hour	Summary of Events and Information	Remarks and references to Appendices
BEUGNEUX	July 31		At 10½ a.m. a draft of 120 men arrived & were distributed to coys on the field. There were practically none members of the Batt⁵. The heavy shelling of the afternoon recommenced but fortunately no shells actually fell on the Batt⁵. The Batt⁵ advanced well to left on the track leading to pt 129. 9r 10m advanced on a bearing of 5½°. Front well clear before the OUCHY LE CHATEAUX – BEUGNEUX Road as far as the rear of the 4 LSH. When the Batt⁵ was halted & turned to the right. Unfortunately the O.C. leading coy gave the command 'quick march' & the 2 coys which had been with the right went off into the dark in the vicinity of the Jerboys 'em	

Army Form C. 2118.

WAR DIARY
or
INTELLIGENCE SUMMARY.

VOL XXXIX July 1915

(Erase heading not required).

Instructions regarding War Diaries and Intelligence Summaries are contained in F.S. Regs., Part II. and the Staff Manual respectively. Title pages will be prepared in manuscript.

Place	Date	Hour	Summary of Events and Information	Remarks and references to Appendices.
BOIS DE BAILLEUL			Statement showing Casualties for period July 22/25	Appendix 6
			do do do July 26/31	do 7
			do do do Aug 1/3	do 8
			Usual monthly statement of strength of Bn.	do 9
			Richard N. Entur Lt Col Cmdg 1/5 R.S.B. Aug 8th 1915	

Secret   Appendix No 1
                                          Vol XXXIX
34th Division
Instructions No 1   Copy No 10

GENERAL SCHEME

1. The Division will carry out an attack on the enemy at an early date (afterwards referred to as "A" day) in conjunction with troops of the 11th French Corps on the Right and the 25th French Division on the Left.

2. **TROOPS.**
The attack will be carried out by the 103rd Infantry Brigade plus 1 company 34th Bn M.G. Corps on the Right and 101st Infantry Brigade plus 1 company 34th Bn M.G. Corps on the Left.

3. The 102nd Infantry Brigade (less 1 Battalion) 2/4th Somerset Light Infantry, 207th, 208th and 209th Field Coy, R.E. and 34th Bn. M.G. Corps less 2 Companies will form a Divisional Reserve. The Field Coys. R.E. and 2/4th Somerset Light Infantry (Pioneers) will be under command of the C.R.E.

4. 1 Battalion of the 102nd Infantry Brigade will be detailed as Corps Reserve. It will be in position in the ravine at the N.W. corner of the BOIS DE BAILLETTE and direct telephonic communication is being arranged by O.C. Div. Signal Coy.

5. The Artillery of the 34th Division supplemented by 2 Regiments of French Field Artillery (total 144 Field Guns and 44 Howitzers) supplemented by Heavy Artillery will support the attack.

STARTING LINE, BOUNDARIES, and OBJECTIVES

6. The approximate line from which the attack will start is shown in dotted BLUE on the attached map.
The actual line will depend on the result of an operation which will be carried out by the 11th French Corps on A minus 1 day with the object of capturing the BUTTE CHALMONT.

7. The limits of the front of the Division are shown in BLUE and the dividing line between Brigades in BLUE DOTTED CHAIN.

8. The first objective is shown in BROWN. With reference to this line it should be understood that it is only intended to show approximately the line which has to be reached and on which a main line of resistance should be formed. A second objective will be ordered as and when the circumstances permit.

ACTION OF TROOPS ON FLANK.

9. (a) The 25th French Division will attack on the left of the 34th Division. The line from which its attack will start is approximately from the N.E. corner of the BOIS DE LA BAILLETTE along the ravine running through Point 148 (1 Kilometre S.E. of MARTIMPRE FARM).

(b) This Division, keeping in touch on its Right with the 34th Division, will attack with its left on the General Line :- station of PLESSIER HULEU — BOIS DE LA TERRE A L'OR — ORME DU GRAND ROZOY. It will take as much advantage of ground as possible to avoid enfilade fire from the BOIS DU PLESSIER. It will skirt GRAND ROZOY on the north and mop up the village when the line of advance has reached a line to the north of the village.

(c) The first objective of this Division is to gain the line :- BOIS DE LA TERRE A L'OR — ORME (DU GRAND) ROZOY — Point 203 — the northern boundary of the 34th Division zone on the eastern end of the feature 203.

(d) A second objective will be ordered according to circumstances.

10. The 11th French Army Corps, on the Right of the 34th Division, will attack from the BUTTE CHALMONT with its left in touch with the 34th Division and establish itself on the line WALLÉE (1,300 yards east of the BUTTE CHALMONT) — BEUGNEUX (exclusive).

PLAN OF ATTACK.

11. The Infantry of the 101st and 103rd Infantry Brigades and the Machine Gun Coys. attached to them will be assembled during the night of the H minus 1 H Day in their attack formation with the leading wave as close to the existing front line East and South of the BOIS DE BAILLETTE as possible.
The position of assembly for the Divisional Reserve will be in the BOIS DE BAILLETTE.

12. The Artillery action will be as follows :-
(a) 1st Phase. - The barrage will open at H hour on the line of the Railway east of the BOIS DE BAILLETTE. It will lift from that line at H plus N minutes. (The number of minutes represented by N depends upon the distance of the front line from the Railway.)
The barrage will advance by lifts of 100 yds every 4 minutes and will continue at this rate until the leading waves of the Infantry have reached the line shown GREEN on

- The barrage will remain East of that line until H plus 2 hours 10 minutes when it will cease.
- During this pause of the barrage at least 2 batteries of Field Guns and 2 Sections field Howitzers (British) will move forward to advanced positions, which must be previously reconnoitred. This artillery will then come under the command of G.O.C. 101st and 103rd Infantry Brigades, 1 Battery field guns & 1 Section of Howitzers to each Brigade.

(B) 2nd Phase. The Infantry will continue their advance at H plus 2 hours 10 minutes and the role of the field artillery will then be to cover and assist the advance of the Infantry, Batteries being moved forward as opportunity offers under orders from Divisional Headquarters.

13. The Infantry will be as described below:-
(a) The disposition of Battalions is left to Brigadiers but troops should be disposed in depth, the principle that each commander has a reserve under his hand being observed. The density of the leading waves must depend upon the amount of opposition met with. These waves must be fed from those in Rear.

B. 1st Phase (i) The advance will commence at H hour, troops passing through the Infantry holding the line. The leading waves will follow the barrage which will consist entirely of H.E. as closely as possible.

(ii) Special parties must be told off beforehand to mop up the trench line which runs Southwards from GRAND ROZOY and which the leading waves must pass over without a pause.

(iii) GRAND ROZOY is inclusive to the 25th French Division. It will be neutralised by Heavy Artillery throughout the advance, and will be encircled and attacked by that Division from the North. The G.O.C. 101st Infantry Brigade will however, detail a flank guard to deal with any attack debouching from the village on his flank. This flank guard must keep well away from the village to avoid the neutralising fire.

IV On reaching the line marked GREEN on the map the leading waves will halt and all units will reorganise under the cover of the protective barrage which will remain down for about 50 minutes. During this pause every effort must be made to replenish supplies of ammunition and push forward machine guns. The neutralising fire on GRAND ROZOY will probably continue during this phase and all troops must be warned that this is our fire and not that of the enemy even though it may be behind them.

(c) 2nd Phase (i) The advance will be resumed at H plus 2 hours 10 minutes and will proceed as before but without a creeping barrage. It is during this period that the closest liaison should be maintained between Infantry and Artillery Commanders that full use may be made of the available artillery support.

(ii) The village of BEUGNEUX and the woods to the west of it constitute the most formidable positions in this phase. Frontal attacks on these positions must be avoided. The G.O.C. 103rd Infantry Brigade will detail a special party to occupy the Hill 158 at the Southern end of the village and will endeavour to encircle the village either by the west using the Copse running south from the road as a screen for the movement, or by both flanks using Hill 158 as a pivot of manoeuvre for movement S.E. of the village. The 101st Infantry Brigade will manoeuvre to turn the Western flank of the woods.

(d) 3rd Phase On reaching approximately the line marked BROWN upon the map a defensive position will be selected and consolidated as quickly as possible. At the same time G.O.C. 103rd Infantry Brigade will push out a strong advance guard in the direction of the BOIS DE BOIS D'ARCY and Point 192 south of SERVENAY. The G.O.C. 101st Infantry Brigade will similarly push out advance guards in the direction of Point 199 and BURY DE BRAS FARM and also along the sheer ...

14. (a) The action of the Divisional Reserve cannot be accurately forecasted. It will be moved into BOIS DE BAILLETTE and subsequently to the line of the road BEUGNEUX – GRAND ROZOY. There it will be held in readiness to capture the village of SERVENAY, to resist counter-attacks or exploit success. The 2/4th Somerset Light Infantry will be held in readiness to be attached to the 102nd Infantry Brigade instead of the battalion detailed as Corps reserve.

The battalion of the 102nd Infantry Brigade detailed as Corps Reserve will be placed in the rear of the Left of the Division but will not pass the SOISSONS – CHATEAU THIERRY road without orders from the Corps Commander which will be issued through Divisional Headquarters.

(B) The 34th Bn. Machine Gun Corps has the 2 coys attached to the 101st and 103rd Infantry Brigades will be handled as opportunity offers.

Those companies may be used during the pause between the 1st and 2nd Phases to deal with counter-attacks during the pause and with hostile opposition as soon as the Infantry advance is resumed. In the 3rd Phase a proportion of guns may be detailed to occupy defensive positions to cover the line consolidated. It must be borne in mind that the ammunition supply will be difficult and that every gun must be brought as far forward as possible before it is brought into action throughout.

J.E. Done Lt.Col. G.S.
34th Division

Issued 1·20 P.M.

Secret.

Copy No. 1 KOSB

103rd Infantry Brigade Order No 225

Reference: maps
OULCHY LE CHATEAU)
FERE EN TARDENOIS) 1/20,000.

Appendice No 2
Vol XXXIX
28th July, 1918.

1. The 34th Division will attack tomorrow morning 29th inst, in conjunction with troops of 11th French Corps on Right and 25th French Division on Left.

2. (A) The attack will be carried out with the 103rd Infantry Brigade plus 1 M.G. Coy on the Right and 101st Infantry Brigade plus 1 M.G. Coy on the Left.
The 102nd Infantry Brigade (less 1 Battn), 2/4th Somerset L.I. 207th, 208th and 209th Field Coy. R.E. and 34th Bn. M.G. Corps (less 2 coys) will form Divisional Reserve.

(B) Brigade Headquarters will be established at S.W. corner of BOIS DE LA BAILLETTE (813.776).
An advanced report centre will be established at point 116. (835.781).
If high ground West of BEUGNEUX is taken, Brigade Hdqrs will move to the wood 848.796.

3. The starting line, boundaries, halts and objectives have already been given to Commanding Officers.

4. The 8th Scottish Rifles will be on the Right. 5th K.O.S.B. on the Left, with the 5th R.S.F. in Brigade Reserve.

5. Each battalion will have 1 M.G. Section (4 Guns) and 1 Section L.T.M. Bty X (2 Guns) attached to it.

6. The action of the Artillery will be as follows:—
The barrage will open at ZERO hour, 200 yards East of existing front line.
The barrage will advance by lifts of 100 yards every 4 minutes and will continue at this rate until the leading waves of Infantry reach the Halting line, shown in GREEN, when a protective barrage will be put down until ZERO plus 1 hour 50 minutes, when the advance will be resumed and there will be no barrage, artillery fire will then be directed by direct observation.
From this time 1 Battery Field Guns and 1 Section Howitzers will be at disposal of O.C. 103rd Infantry Brigade.

7. The action of the Infantry will be as follows:-
(1) The advance will commence at ZERO hour, troops passing through the French Infantry holding the line. The leading waves will follow the barrage as close as possible.
(2) Each battalion will detail one platoon beforehand to mop up the trench line which runs Southwards from GRAND ROZOY and which the leading waves must pass over without a pause.
(3) At the Halting Place (marked GREEN on map) all troops will be re-organised.
(4) Both woods to the West of BEUGNEUX and the village of BEUGNEUX will be turned from the North and South respectively.
(5) After BEUGNEUX has been cleared, troops will be re-organised in the valley to the East of it.
(6) When the final objective is reached, it will be consolidated at once in depth.

8. O.C's 5TH K.O.S.B. and 8TH Scottish Rifles may call on Brigade Reserve direct for assistance in case of necessity. Otherwise they will not be employed without reference to GOC 103rd Infantry Brigade.

9. Such of the Brigade Reserve as have not been engaged will take up a position in the valley East of BEUGNEUX and will be responsible for protection of Right Flank.

10. Patrols will be pushed East and South towards BOIS D'ARCY and Point 192.

11. Battalions will detail special parties to prevent stragglers.

12. All prisoners will be sent direct to Brigade Hdqrs.

13. Each unit will send a guide to Brigade Hdqrs. after dark tomorrow night 29TH inst., to guide their transport with rations &c.

14. A Dump of S.A.A. etc is being formed in vicinity of Brigade Hdqrs. which will be pushed forward on Pack mules if urgently required. Also in vicinity of Brigade Hdqrs. will be 4 Riding horses per Battalion which will be used for liaison purposes if the nature of the fighting permits.

15. Transport of units will be held ready to move at the shortest notice tomorrow 29th inst.

16. Watches will be synchronised at place of assembly and at 2 am. 29th inst.

17. Medical arrangements will be notified later.

18. Acknowledge.

R.W Rutherford.
Captain.
Brigade Major.
103rd Infantry Brigade.

Issued through Signals at 7.45 P.M.

Brigade Wire B.M. 176   Appendix 9.
                                  Vol XXXIX.
                               29th July 1918.

5th Bn. K.O.S.B.

The 102nd Bde will attack at 2.30 P.M. and will endeavour to reach the original objective of the 101st Bde, attacking BEAUGNEUX from the north aaa The 103rd Bde will attack at same hour and endeavour to turn BEAUGNEUX from the South and reach the original objective aaa The barrage line will be roughly HILL 189 - 122 - village of BEAUGNEUX and 158. The barrage will lift at 2.30 P.M. aaa Written orders have not been received from Divn and in all probability will not be in time to issue to units aaa Acknowledge

From   103rd Inf Bde
         12.20 P.M.

                               Signed R.W. Rutherford

Secret.

103rd Infantry Brigade Order No. 226.

Reference Maps
OULCHY LE CHATEAU
FERE EN TARDENOIS } 1/20,000

Appendix IV
Vol XXXIX
31st July, 1918.

1. The 34th Division will resume the attack tomorrow morning 1st August.
The objective, Divisional and Brigade boundaries and forming up place are shown on the attached map.
ZERO hour will be 5 am.
(a) The 30th and 11th French Corps are attacking at the same time.
30 Tanks are co-operating and they will probably cross the Brigade front from the Left on approaching the BROWN line.
(b) The 103rd Infantry Brigade will be on the Right and the 101st Infantry Brigade on the Left (with 4th Royal Sussex Regt as Right Battalion) and 102nd Infantry Brigade as Divisional Reserve.

2. The 8th Scottish Rifles will take over as soon as it is dark tonight 31st inst, the front at present held by 1/7th Cheshire Regt up to the inter Brigade Boundary (with exception of their forward posts, which will remain in their present position).

3. ACTION OF INFANTRY
(a) The Infantry will advance at ZERO hour. The 103rd Infantry Brigade will turn the village of BEUGNEUX from the South and the 101st Infantry Brigade from the North.
(b) The 103rd Infantry Brigade will attack with the 5th K.O.S.B. on the Right, 5th A.&S.H. on the Left and 8th Scottish Rifles in Brigade Reserve.
(c) As soon as it is dark tonight 31st inst Battalions will move to assembly positions as shown on attached map.
(d) The inter Battalion Boundary as soon as troops are East of BEUGNEUX will be exactly half the Brigade frontage – 5th A.&S.H. on the Northern half and 5th K.O.S.B. on Southern half.
(e) As soon as the high ground North and South of BEUGNEUX has been taken, 2 Coys. 8th Scottish Rifles will go through and into the village, the remaining 2 coys 8th Scottish Rifles following the 5th A.&S.H. and 5th K.O.S.B. and are at their c.o.s

The 2 coys 8th Scottish Rifles following 5th A&SH and 5th K.O.S.B. if they have not been called upon when the high ground south of BEUGNEUX is taken, will assemble just East of the village when they will be joined by the other 2 coys as soon as they have cleared the village.

(F) On reaching the objective, Battalions will at once consolidate and occupy it in depth.

4. ACTION OF MACHINE GUNS

The machine Guns attached to the Brigade will remain in their present positions and cover the advance with overhead fire until the objective is taken, when one section will report to each battalion and one section will remain in its present position till further orders.

5. ACTION OF ARTILLERY

Our Artillery during the night will carry out a bombardment till 4.15 am when it will become intense and will continue so until ZERO hour, when a creeping barrage will commence at the rate of 3 minutes per 100 metres.

One battery Field Guns and 2 Hows. will be at the disposal of G.O.C. 103rd Infantry Brigade for close support work.

6. Two Light Trench Mortars will be with each Battalion.

7. On the objective being taken the 127th French Division will pass through the 34th Division and continue the advance.

8. O.C. 5th K.O.S.B. will maintain close liaison with the French Troops on his Right.

9. Battalions will report by wire when complete in assembly positions.

10. Watches will be synchronised this afternoon and again later if possible.

11. Brigade Hqrs. will remain present position until objective is taken, after which they will move to BOIS DE BEUGNEUX.

12. ACKNOWLEDGE.

R W Rutherford.
Captain
Brigade Major
103rd Infantry Brigade

Issued through Signals at 2.45 P.M.

WAR - DIARY
of
1/5th King's Own Scottish Borderers
from 1-8-18 — 31-8-18

Vol - XL -

WAR DIARY
or
INTELLIGENCE SUMMARY.
(Erase heading not required.)

Army Form C. 2118.

Vol ~~XX~~ ~~IX~~

August 1918

Place	Date	Hour	Summary of Events and Information	Remarks and references to Appendices
BEUGNEUX	Aug. 1st 18		The Bn was in position as about 12.30 a.m. At 0445 the barrage of field guns was put down in front of our line. At 0445 the Brookes replied with machine guns. At 0449 our barrage lifted to the first line & the support Coy went forward. At 0457 Bn. H.Q. also advanced. The smoke from our barrage also started in front. The mist in the morning just was so thick that nothing could be seen beyond about 15 yards & objects had to direct by compass. The front line advanced with its left on the S.E. corner of Hill 158. At any rate a portion of D Coy cleared the enemy flanking trench along behind to took about 20 prisoners. The front line then screwed to its left & went up the westerly of Hill 158 & cleared the aerodrome wood. The A&C H meantime had gone for the [wood] hill 15-S from the south west. The left line then went up the rear end of the village & captured the left [prond] on a line about through 6191 on the right. They just missed the actual objective but here & prise kept up & M G fire from the flank.	MINDEN DAY

Army Form C. 2118.

WAR DIARY
or
INTELLIGENCE SUMMARY.
(Erase heading not required).

Vol XI
August 1918

Place	Date	Hour	Summary of Events and Information	Remarks and references to Appendices.
BEUGNEUX Aug 1st			Negotiation took later with the French to the right & reinforced this attack. Owner of the wood & were by tops or else pushed with a M.G. At this point a platoon under 2/Lt GRAHAM "A" Coy came in from the right & captured this true including H.Q. & prisoners. As Bn H.Q. reaches the clearing on the E. side of hill 158 it found about 100 H.T.S.H. who had come over 158 that had lost nearly all their officers. 2/Lts FRENCH & GILLESPIE were ordered to take them on & with a cheer they dashed up the hill towards the main objective. H.Q. then moved up to the quarry in 6095 & was able to report on the position to Brigade. The parties under 2/Lts FRENCH & GILLESPIE captured about 50 prisoners including 2 officers & a number of machine guns. Brigade HQ/1454 & ordinate from H.Q. moved up & consolidated on a line 6458/6291 joining up with the HEREFORDS & LOYAL NORTH LANCS on the left. The two front lines ag¹ "A" Coy came on through the aerodrome taking about 30 more prisoners & dried up with the front in the hill. The French meantime making the aerodrome secure.	The support Coy also went to attack the Bn HQ.

A.P. & S.D., Alex./2009/50325A/III:17/5M. W.M. & Co.

WAR DIARY or INTELLIGENCE SUMMARY

Army Form C. 2118.

Vol XI. August 1915

Place	Date	Hour	Summary of Events and Information	Remarks and references to Appendices.
BEUGNEUX	Aug 1st		The Right Flank on the hill did not appear secure & a company of the Serbian Rifles was placed there to protect it. The Consolidation was done in two lines with Lewis Guns pushed out on to the forward slopes. At this time there was considerable M.G. fire coming from the North & Right Flank. Soon however the French were seen advancing on the right & reaching the outskirts of SERNAY. They also advanced on the left so far as COURDEUX & the Bois DE BEHER. Consolidation was carried on & as there seemed no likelihood of a counter attack, orders were to organise. C & A in the Front line with D & B in support respectively. The A&SH were sent in to the left, & as they had no officer M.I. FRENCH remained with them. At about 07:30 the enemy commenced to shell the area. Orders came from Brigade at 14:00 that the line was to be held by the N.F.'s & S.R. with the A&SH withdrawn to the sunken line in S.9.9.8 & that the brigade was to advance to the original objective	

Army Form C. 2118.

WAR DIARY
or
INTELLIGENCE SUMMARY.
(Erase heading not required.)

Vol XL August 1918

Place	Date	Hour	Summary of Events and Information	Remarks and references to Appendices
BEUGNEUX	1918 Aug 1st		It was reported to Brigade that the HEREFORDS had failed to reach hill 199 & had been forced to withdraw & that it would require a Divisional arm for the whole line to advance. At 6.15 pm orders for a general advance were received, the an artillery barrage, which advanced by 4 minute bounds of 100 yards commencing at 7.4 pm. Behind this barrage the line advanced. The Bn. negotiated in being in a (cheers) slope of the hill & had few casualties, but the battalions on the left suffered severely. The new line was reached & consolidated & the Bn settled down for the night.	
	2nd	O.K.	In the morning it was found that even for the Bn & the SR on the left were not occupying the correct objective and Coys pushed forward about 300 to the line through Pt. 172. Orders were received about 12 noon that the Division would be required to advance & support the French, who had pushed through us. At about 6.30 pm orders were issued to concentrate at the Black huts south of BEUGNEUX with Bn HQ at the Quarry 59.9.8. This move was effected.	

Army Form C. 2118.

WAR DIARY
or
INTELLIGENCE SUMMARY.
(Erase heading not required.)

Vol XL
August 1918

Place	Date	Hour	Summary of Events and Information	Remarks and references to Appendices
BEUGNEUX	August 1918 3rd		The Bn. spent the day in rest. At 5.30 p.m. a special parade was held at 103 Bde. HQ & French decorations were presented by the Divisional Commander. Bn. Awards. No. 241198 Pte. John Joseph O'HARE — MEDAILLE MILITAIRE & CROIX de GUERRE Citn. d'Armée Lt. Col. R.K. COULSON — CROIX de GUERRE Citation d'Armée 2/Lt. O.W.F. RICHARDSON (wounded) — do A/Cpl. John KEVAN — do — Martyr d'Armée SPECIAL ORDER OF THE DAY by 34th DIVISION Appendix I	
DAMMARTIN	4th		During the night orders were received to move the next morning at 9.15 a.m. and the battalion marched to the OMS Road at 24.78 & embussed for DAMMARTIN just north of PARIS. This was reached at 7 p.m. & the battalion went into billets.	
Do	5		Day spent in rest & cleaning up. Mueller and transport which had gone 46 miles in two days marching (via BOURGET & MOURILLY SUR OURCQ) reported.	

Army Form C. 2118.

WAR DIARY
or
INTELLIGENCE SUMMARY.
(Erase heading not required.)

Vol XL
August 1918

Instructions regarding War Diaries and Intelligence Summaries are contained in F.S. Regs., Part II. and the Staff Manual respectively. Title pages will be prepared in manuscript.

Place	Date	Hour	Summary of Events and Information	Remarks and references to Appendices
DAMMARTIN	August 6		Bn received orders to entrain at 7am for the British area but it was afterwards delayed till 11.52 a.m. Bn marched to the station at ST MAARD & entrained	
WORMHOUT	7		Arrived at 2 pm & marched to billets in WORMHOUT. 2 Officers rejoined from hospital 2/Lt KAYE & 2/Lt MILLER + HOOD 1 Officer rejoined from hospital	
	8		Draft of 62 O.R. rejoined from hospital leave S/Lt JOHNSTON 1 Officer returned from hospital 2/Lt JOHNSTON	Brittain to Lydern '3 Class 2/Lt BURN Sp. CAIN Moss & Givens 2/L Class 2/Lt T. GRAHAM Capp McKay Sgt Brady Cpl J.S. Graham
	9		Commenced training. Presentation of Promotions 2/Lt W. GRAHAM	
	10		1 Officer to hospital 1 Officer rejoined from hospital 2 OR leave	2/Lt T. McGILL Capt McBRYDE Diaries
	11	Nil	Draft of 247 O.R. joined from U.K. Billetted by themselves in new billets. Trained as above. This Draft all men of 18th year of age. Smart Lads. Distributed new Draft to companies.	

WAR DIARY or INTELLIGENCE SUMMARY

Army Form C. 2118.

Vol XL August 1918

Place	Date	Hour	Summary of Events and Information	Remarks and references to Appendices
WORMHOUDT	Aug 12 1918		5 Officers joined from 3rd K.O.S.B. 2/Lt. J.T.PRIOR	All from DANDHURST R.W. LOVE, J. HOPE, G.D. THOMSON, W.G. MADINGLEY
	13		1 Officer returned from hospital 2/Lt. W. McDONALD	
			1 Officer admitted to hospital Capt. W.H.TURNER M.C.	
			Bn marched at 8.30 for ST. JAN DER BEIZEN a considerable number of new drafts fell out on march. 16 sentences 6 to 2H[?] hard labour for 2 days	
			2 Lt. VR 2/Lt Ventris on team to Capt. Officers Wing a week	Lt R.J.RICHARDSON 2/Lt H.H.WHITE
	14		2 Officers sick to hospital	
			1 Officer joined for duty	Lt I. McHARDY
			appointed Bn acting Signalling Officer	
			1 Officer proceeded on leave to U.K.	Lt HOGARTH

Army Form C. 2118.

WAR DIARY
or
INTELLIGENCE SUMMARY.
(Erase heading not required.)

Vol XI
August 1918

Instructions regarding War Diaries and Intelligence Summaries are contained in F. S. Regs., Part II. and the Staff Manual respectively. Title pages will be prepared in manuscript.

Place	Date 1918	Hour	Summary of Events and Information	Remarks and references to Appendices
JAN TER BIEZEN	Aug 15.		1 Officer returned from leave in U.K. Capt V. McM. GILMOUR	
DIRTY BUCKET AREA	16	8.45	Bn marched at 8.45 to DIRTY BUCKET AREA. Lt. Linsley to take over with companies. Remainder of transport bivy'd nets Capt behind Bn. 1 Officer joined for duty from U.K. 2/Lt WALLMAN	
	17.	A.K.	1 Officer joined for duty from U.K. - 2/Lt. MUNRO.	
	18.	A.K.	2 Officers joined for duty from U.K. - 2/Lt. E. CRAWFORD, BAIRNSFATHER. 2/Lt. Duke of Wellington's Regt. in left.	
	19.	A.K.	Batt. received orders to relieve 1/6H sect of brigade frontage at POTISZE. Officer reconnoitred the line. Advance party of 16 officers per coy, I.C.S.M. per coy and 1 N.C.O. per platoon moved up in the evening.	

Army Form C. 2118.

WAR DIARY
or
INTELLIGENCE SUMMARY.
(Erase heading not required.)

Place	Date	Hour	Summary of Events and Information	Remarks and references to Appendices
YPRES — LEFT SECTOR 24.	23/24		Relief carried out. Colonel Corkran proceeding on leave to PARIS, the Batt. was under the command of Major Beara, M.C. The 5th A.&S.H. were on the right. Liaison obtained with 2nd Belgian Grenadier Regt. on left by liaison posts, and a liaison officer attached to the battalion H.Q.	
	24	2.30— 4.30 A.M.	Enemy bombarded our front and support line with about 700 rounds — 77's, 4"2 and a few 5"9.	
		8.30p.m.	One prisoner captured by "B" Company patrol. He stated that he was one of a party who set out the previous night to raid our trenches, and that the raid had been dispersed by the German artillery firing short and scattering their own men.	
	25		26 Officer joined for duty from 11.K.—2/Lt. EDGELL, PURVES	
	25/26		Batt. relieved in front line by 8th Lancs. Rifles. Moved	

WAR DIARY
or
INTELLIGENCE SUMMARY.
(Erase heading not required.)

Army Form C. 2118.

Place	Date	Hour	Summary of Events and Information	Remarks and references to Appendices
YPRES			into Brigade reserve in the YPRES and CANAL defences. Batt. H.Q. in EAST ramparts of YPRES.	A.K.
29th	27th	9.30pm	Batt: supplied working parties for Reserve line trip trenches	A.K.
29th	28	10pm	Relieve by 29 D.L.I. and marched back to BRIELEN Reserve line.	
29th	29th		Batt: left BRIELEN Reserve line at 8pm & marched via YLAMERTINGHE station & OUDERDOM to SCHERPENBERG Reserve Area at ZEVECOTEN.	A.K.
	30th		Preparations made to relieve 26th Royal Fus. in left sector of 129 to 88 line (immediately East of the SCHERPENBERG) Advance parties for relief sent up. Bivouac reported evacuated by the enemy. Batt: always to hold itself in readiness to move at short notice.	A.K.

Army Form C. 2118.

WAR DIARY
or
INTELLIGENCE SUMMARY.
(Erase heading not required.)

Place	Date	Hour	Summary of Events and Information	Remarks and references to Appendices
LEUCEOTW	31st		Enemy evacuated Mt KEMMEL. Orders received at 8.45 a.m. for Battn to move to GORDON Rt on N. Western slopes of KEMMEL in support of 9th S.R. Raind hard.	AK.
			Statement showing strength of Bn Casualties etc :-	APP 1

Andrew Kay Capt
A/ Major
Comdg 1/5th KOSB

31st Sept 1918 -

7th Kings Own (Scottish Borderers)

Appendix No.1 to War Diary for month of August 1918

		Off.	O.Rs.
(1)	Strength of unit 1-8-18	31	491
(2)	" " " 31-8-18	40	484
(3)	Sick to Hospital	9	90
(4)	Reinforcements	12	392
(5)	Transferred to U.K.	3	—
(6)	Casualties Wounded	—	6

1/5th Kings Own Scottish Borderers
Casualty Return from midnight
31st July to noon 3rd Aug 1918.

Officers:-

      Killed
2/Lt W. ROBINSON 3rd KOSB
                      1-8-18

      Wounded-
2/Lt O.W.F RICHARDSON 5 KOSB 1-8-18
  2 McK.D. FLINT M.M. 6th HLI   "
      MISSING.
Lt G.G. CARMICHAEL 4/4 KOSB   "

OTHER RANKS.

    Killed   25

    Wounded   112

    Missing   24

9-8-18   Lt Col
       Com-dg 1/5 KOSBs

Appendix 6

1/5 KOSB Casualty Return
from noon July 22nd to noon July 28th

	Killed	Wounded	Missing
Officers		Capt & adjt T.D Craig 24-7-18	
OR's	1	13	Nil

7-8-18-

Lt Col.
Comdg 1/5ᵗʰ KOSB

Appendix Appendix No - 10.
War Diary for July 1918.

Strength of Unit 30/6/18.
              Offrs   OR's
              39   826.

Strength of Unit 9-8-18.
              Offrs   OR's
              31   491

Casualties:-
              Officers   OR's
Killed   3   43
Wounded   8   339
Missing   1   51
              12   433

Sick to Hospital.
              Officers   OR's
              5   104

Reinforcements.
              Offrs   OR's
              4   188

[Stamp: 1/8th BATTALION KING'S OWN SCOTTISH BORDERERS]

Appendix 9

1/5 King's own Scottish Borderers

Casualty Return from noon 28th July
to midnight 31st July - 1918

Officers Killed — Date

2/Lieut. S. ROBERTSON 3rd/KOSB. 29.7.18.
" A.R. JOHNSTON 5th H.L.I. 29.7.18.

Officers Wounded — Date

Capt. J. McGEORGE 5 KOSB. 29.7.18
2/Lt J. ALSTON 5 H.L.I. 29.7.18
" J. WEIR 3rd KOSB. 29.7.18
" J. KNOWLES " 29.7.18
" H.M. BLYTH " 29.7.18

Officers Missing.

Nil.

O.R.'s

Killed	Wounded	Missing
19	214	29

9-8-18.   Lt Col
Comdg 1/5th KOSB.

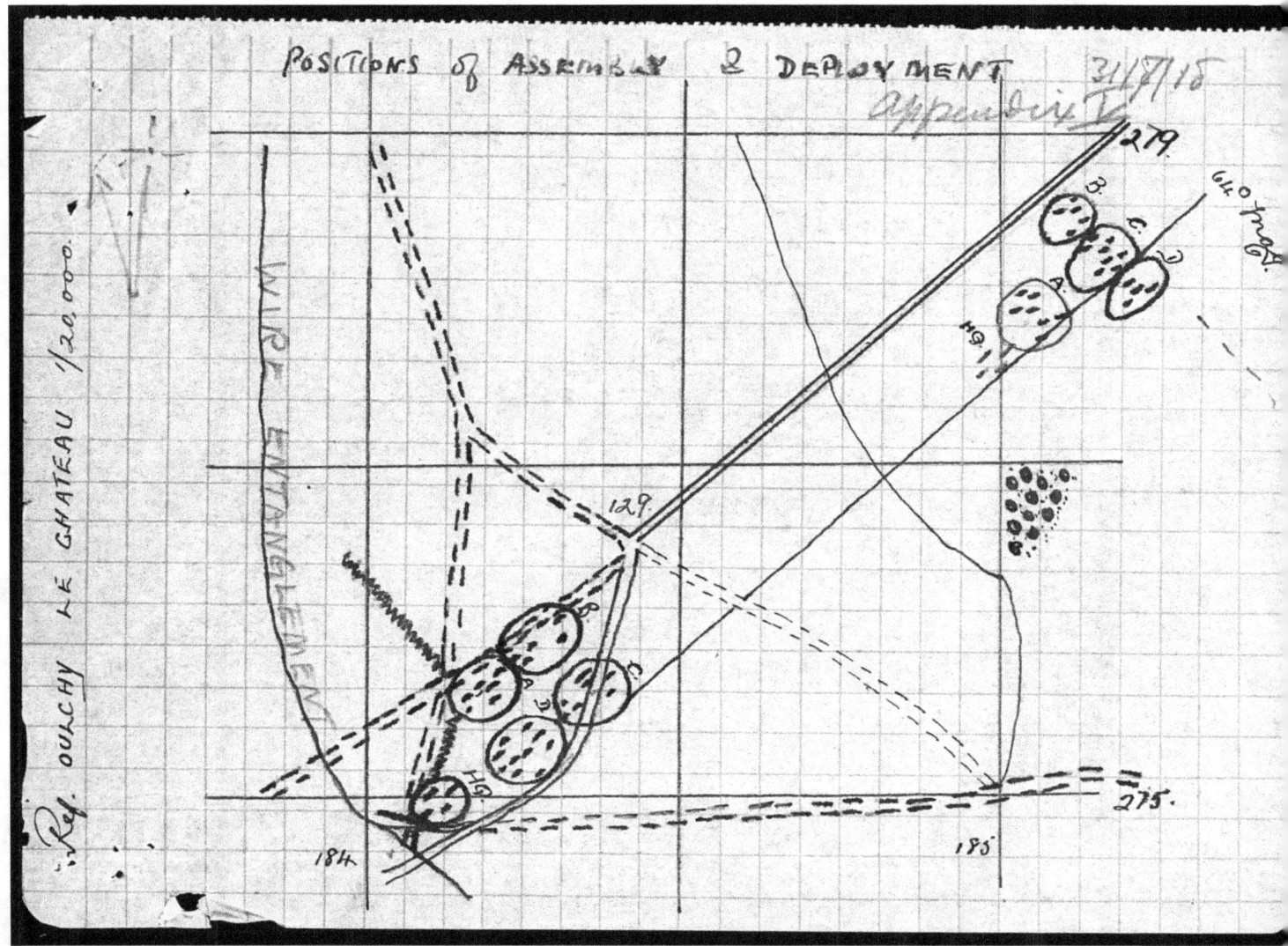

HQ.
103: Inf. Bde.

R 7/3

Herewith WAR DIARY of the unit under my command for month ending 30th Sept. 1918.

7/10/18.

Richard N. Curlson
Lt. Colonel,
Comdg. 5 KOSB

CONFIDENTIAL. U.26

13.W.
3 sheets.

WAR DIARY.
of
1/5th King's Own Scottish Borderers.
from
1-9-18 to 30-9-18.
Vol. XLI.

Army Form C. 2118.

WAR DIARY
or
INTELLIGENCE SUMMARY.
(Erase heading not required.)

VOL XLI
September 1918

Place	Date	Hour	Summary of Events and Information	Remarks and references to Appendices
KEMMEL	Sept 1st		Continued to rain till dawn. Ground in very bad condition & only a fact. Several obstacles in the shape of wires, barbed wire entanglements, shell holes & gun emplacements lay across the front. Orders were received during the night 31st Aug/1st Sept the 8th S.R. to relieve units of 129th Regt. in the VIERSTRAAT line on the S.E. side of Mont KEMMEL by 5.30 am. Supported by 2 Coys of the Batt. Batt. HQ and 3 Coys of the Batt. until the remaining 2 Coys of the Batt. moved up & remain on the Mont-western slopes of KEMMEL till an advance was made. Bn HQ & D+C Coys took up a position in the vicinity of KEMMEL shelters at 4.30 am. A+D Coys following the 8th S.R. took up a position in support of the Batt. on SE slopes of KEMMEL at 5.30 am. The 8th S.R. about to advance at 9 am. D+A Coys to occupy the position vacated by the night-fort Coy — C+B Coys to occupy the position	

Army Form C. 2118.

WAR DIARY
or
INTELLIGENCE SUMMARY.
(Erase heading not required.)

VOL XLI September 1915

Place	Date	Hour	Summary of Events and Information	Remarks and references to Appendices
KEMMEL (LINDENHOEK)	1st		Of the left front & left support Coys of the 8=S=R respectively, so that "Batt" advanced the "Batt" did not know the VIERSTRAAT support line during the day, as the advance of the leading half of the Brigade was delayed owing to NEUVE EGLISE on the right flank remaining in the hands of the enemy.	
do	2nd		The Batt remained in the same position during the night of 1st/2nd. No further advance being permitted by the 8=S=R. He Qrs established with those of the 8=S=R on the LINDENHOEK Rd near DAYLIGHT Corner. Orders received during the morning for 2 Coys of the Batt to advance at 3 P.M. and occupy RESERVE DUGOUTS. A barrage to be put down on the enemy's trenches (MESSINES ridge) from 2:55 to 3:15 p.m. at PECKHAM and SPANBROEK MOLEN	

Army Form C. 2118.

WAR DIARY
or
INTELLIGENCE SUMMARY.

Vol XLI September 1915

(Erase heading not required.)

Place	Date	Hour	Summary of Events and Information	Remarks and references to Appendices
KEMMEL (LINDENHOEK Rd)	Sept 2		The 2/4th Queens on the left of the 8th S.R. were relieved by the 1/4th in STORE F.M. C & D Coys allied to make this advance. These coys moving via LINDENHOEK deployed on the Northern side of the SPY Ft – STORE Ft road. D Coy leading with C Coy in support at 3 pm the leading Coy advanced – a hostile barrage was at once put down on the road at the same time the enemy opened M.G. fire from the direction of STORE F.M. which enfiladed our line & stopped the advance. It was then apparent to the leading Coy Com^{dr}. that the 2/4th Queens had not, as far as known, held by the leading Coy of the 2/4th Queens had not, as far as known, advanced as that Battⁿ. had been told. A report to this effect was sent to the Brigade and arrangements made	

WAR DIARY or INTELLIGENCE SUMMARY.

Army Form C. 2118.

Vol LXI September 1918

(Erase heading not required.)

Instructions regarding War Diaries and Intelligence Summaries are contained in F.S. Regs., Part II. and the Staff Manual respectively. Title pages will be prepared in manuscript.

Place	Date	Hour	Summary of Events and Information	Remarks and references to Appendices
KEMMEL (HINDENBURG)	2		A few rounds of H.E. PECKHAM and SPANBROEKMOLEN craters fired on at 5.15 am & 11.30 am. C & D Coys ended their move forward at dusk. Then was carried out and a line taken up by C & D Coys in front of REGENTS DUGOUTS about 10 a.m. Touch being gained with the 2/4th to our left of the Byr- and Estab- sent back to the left of the 2nd S.R. who had not advanced at this time. Orders received during the evening that the Brigade would be relieved by 102nd Inf Bde. Guides from Coys went to "Batt" HdQrs for relieving units. 2nd Chesh Regt arrived at Bn HdQrs about one hour and two Coys of that Batt" relieving the "Batt" — the remaining two Coys relieving the 2nd S.R.	

WAR DIARY
or
INTELLIGENCE SUMMARY.

Army Form C. 2118.

Vol XXI September 1918

(Erase heading not required.)

Place	Date	Hour	Summary of Events and Information	Remarks and references to Appendices
SCHERPENBERG	3		Relf of Bn' by 2 coys 7th Cheshires completed at 2 AM	
			Batt'n marched back by coys to SCHERPENBERG Reserve Area	
			Batt'n moved during the evening to new	
			Area to be employed by way of	
			to the B.20025 - KEMMEL area from	
RIMMEL	4		Batt'n moved to BRULOOZE - KEMMEL area and proceeded	
			to relieve the GORDONS and BRULOOZE - BUTTERFLY FM "D"	
do	5		Day spent in erecting shelters & dugouts	
do	6-7-8		R.E. found working parties for the R.E. on the works and	
			WERSTRAAT Line hair half = H.Q.D.N companied	
			L/102 R.M.COULDR went to a Commanding Officers Course at	
			Wisques when the day had	
SC.02m	9		Batt'n marched to G.S.E201 Reserve Area & billets	

WAR DIARY or INTELLIGENCE SUMMARY.

Army Form C. 2118.

WT IXI September 1918

Place	Date	Hour	Summary of Events and Information	Remarks and references to Appendices
STEENVOORDE	Sept 10		Batt'n marched to STEENVOORDE station and entrained by half batt'ns for ST MOMELIN. Detrained at ST MOMELIN and marched to HELLEBROUCQ	
HELLEBROUCQ	11		Batt'n arrived in the early hours of the morning at HELLEBROUCQ where it was billeted.	
	12		Training commenced	
	13		Actg Brig Comd saw Batt'n training	
	14		Lt Col Courbier attended for course at WISQUES	
	15		Church Parade at EPERLECQUES. Capt Commander (LtGen Sir H Watts) inspected Battalion Work.	Lt Col R F Gillen D.S.O. Sgt W S Grant D.C.M. Sgt Caine M.M. Sgt Carran M.M. Pte Buchanan M.M. Pte O'Hare M.M. Cpl Strange D.M.
	16		Brigade Communication Scheme	

Army Form C. 2118.

WAR DIARY
or
INTELLIGENCE SUMMARY.
(Erase heading not required.)

Vol. XLI September 1915

Place	Date	Hour	Summary of Events and Information	Remarks and references to Appendices
HELLEBROUCQ	Sept 17		Coy Training & Musketry. Co. hosted O.C.s & Lieuts of Bn. front Co. at WYTSCHAETE	
	18		Demonstration to Officers & N.C.Os on 19th Corps School of methods of training a platoon.	
	19		Coy Training in arms round billets. Transport turned to DIVIZEE ARNEEQUES ARNEKE	
	20		Bn. moved to Abele. Transport also came there. Capt Weir Manchester Regt reported to Bn. as Quartermaster	
	21		moved into line opposite WYTSCHAETE. Relieved 15th Hants. Relief completed by 11.15 p.m. A + B Coys in front line. C + D in support. Trenches little more than slit holes.	
WYTSCHAETE	22		Quiet. No movement allowed during day in front of Bn. HQrs. Time repaired in places during night.	
	23		Quiet during day. At night our line was advanced in accordance with Operation Orders. The platoon covering the advance of the left Coy. under	

WAR DIARY
or
INTELLIGENCE SUMMARY.
(Erase heading not required.)

Army Form C. 2118.

Vol. XLI September 1918.

Place	Date	Hour	Summary of Events and Information	Remarks and references to Appendices
WYTSCHAETE	23		2/Lt. Cairns was 3 times attacked under a barrage of rifle-grenades & m.g. fire by a fighting patrol of approximately 40 Germans. The covering Platoon each time repulsed the attack with Lewis gun & rifle fire. 2/Lt. E. P. Dickie reported to Battn. after U.K. leave. 7 men were wounded by rifle-grenades.	
	24		2/Lts. G. B. Jenkens & A. B. Johnston proceeded to hospital. Posts in new line improved during night	
	25-26		Front line positions improved by night	
	27	8 p.m.	Battalion H.Q. moved to left front Coy H.Q. at O.1.c.0.8. Liaison officer joined from R.F.A, M.G, & L.T.M. this night with men in 3rd Quarters. Left front Coy. ("D") withdrew all posts east of line 1st B in BOLLARDBEEK to O.7.b.1.9 back to old FRENCH TRENCH by 4.30 A.M.	

Army Form C. 2118.

WAR DIARY
or
INTELLIGENCE SUMMARY.
(Erase heading not required.)

Vol. XLI, Sept. 1918.

Place	Date	Hour	Summary of Events and Information	Remarks and references to Appendices
WYTSCHAETE	28.		"D" Coy. formed up as a front line 2/Lt CAIRNS' platoon and in support of 2/Lt HYSLOP's platoon in line with 11th A.&S.H. to the left. The 3 right posts of "D" Coy. made 2/Lt. WALLBANK were formed up on the line of three 3 posts. At 5.25 A.M. our barrage came down along the front of old FRENCH TRENCH and along Light Ry. for 200ˣ to the WEST of broad gauge railway. The barrage after 5 minutes advanced at rate of 100ˣ each 3 minutes. At 5.25 A.M. 2/Lt CAIRNS advanced up to the barrage and followed it up to PICCADILLY F.M. supported by 2/Lt. HYSLOP, taking prisoner 1 Officer and 38 O.R. and 2 M.Gs. before the 11th A.&S.H. entered the farm when the barrage	

WAR DIARY or INTELLIGENCE SUMMARY

Army Form C. 2118.

Vol XLI Sept 1918

Place	Date	Hour	Summary of Events and Information	Remarks and references to Appendices
WYTSCHAETE	28		on the left came level with that on right Rgt. at 5.40 A.M. both Coys advanced. 2/Lt WALLBANK mopped up trench on Left railway taking 9 prisoners and 1 M.G. He then took up position on N.E. end of BOIS QUARANTE. 2/Lt CAIRNS and Lt HYSLOP in 2 lines E&W of road at O.8.a.6.6. At 5.40 × Capt GILMOUR, C Coy, sent out 1 platoon as a patrol to take up the objective above mentioned at N.E. corner of BOIS QUARANTE. At 7.30 Capt GILMOUR sent out another platoon supported by a second platoon with orders to push through BOIS QUARANTE at O.7.c&d The patrol took up a position at about O.7.d. 3.6.	

Army Form C. 2118.

WAR DIARY
— or —
INTELLIGENCE SUMMARY.
(Erase heading not required.)

Vol. XLI Sept. 1918

Place	Date	Hour	Summary of Events and Information	Remarks and references to Appendices
WYTSCHAETE.	28		At 7.30 Lt. REID and 2/Lt. E.P. DICKIE and 16 signallers & 2 runners went to establish an advanced report centre about O.T.6.4.4. This was in position at 8.15. At this time information was received that a patrol of 5th A.&S.H. had pushed out to GRAND BOIS but had been driven back. Orders were sent to Capt. GILMOUR & 2/Lt. ALSTON to push on. Meanwhile "B" Coy. had moved out in 3 lines & had advanced its front line having reached O.8.a.central. The right platoon of "D" Coy. pushed on to O.8.a.6.2. "C" Coy. then pushed out to LOUWAEGE FM. but were held up. Patrols meantime were pushing out in front but no real progress was made. At 4 P.M. a message was received from Capt. GILMOUR timed 3 P.M. stating "C" Coy. H.Q.	

Army Form C. 2118.

WAR DIARY
or
INTELLIGENCE SUMMARY.
(Erase heading not required.)

Vol. XLI. Sept. 1918

Place	Date	Hour	Summary of Events and Information	Remarks and references to Appendices
WYTSCHAETE.	28.		at O.7.c.5.0 with "B" Coy. "D" Coy. facing EAST along road ST. ELOI — OOSTAERT. "C" Coy. being just north of GATTEAU FM. "B" Coy. at RLY. crossing and "D" Coy. just north of them. H.A. & S.H. in GRAND BOIS near RENTY FM. one platoon of "C" in LOUWAEGE FM., 1 section M.G.s between O.7.c.6.9. and O.7.6.9.0. Heavy M.G. fire from about 4 guns were coming from DOME HOUSE and also from ridge about MARTENS FM. To expected a barrage (artillery) on this ridge. Bde. arranged for this at 4.45 & other not received accordingly. Unfortunately before the barrage came down 4 M.G.s had subdued the fire from the DOME HOUSE — EN DER JAEGER CABARET ridge, and "D" Coy. & the 5th. A & S.H. had pushed in and captured repeatedly DOME HOUSE & ZERO FARM. At 4.45 came the barrage was very heavy and forced our troops to withdraw from the	

Army Form C. 2118.

WAR DIARY
or
INTELLIGENCE SUMMARY.
(Erase heading not required.)

Vol XLI. Sept. 1918.

Place	Date	Hour	Summary of Events and Information	Remarks and references to Appendices
WYTSCHAETE	28		positions gained, and there were 9 casualties. The Brigade then took up the BLUE LINE, – PICADILLY, ZERO HOUSE, NORTHERN BRICKSTACKS.	
		6.30 P.M.	orders arrived for an advance at 7 P.M. on DOME HOUSE & BANDULLE F.M. with a barrage on that line. The orders for this attack reached the troops after the barrage had finished &	
			Unfortunately again a few shells landed amongst our own troops. C.O. then saw the Brig and consolidation commenced on BLUE LINE.	
		8 P.M.	orders were received to make good the line DOME HOUSE – BANDULLE F.M. & this was done at 4 A.M.	Batt. Operation Order No.10. Appendix T.
			Casualties 1 Officer killed, 1 wounded. 8 N.C.O.R. 2 killed. 40 O.R. 2 missing 40 wounded	
	29	9.30 P.M.	Batt. H.O. was moved to LOUVIAEGE F.M. and orders were then received to take up new H.Q. at DAMM STRASSE & for the Batt. to take up the BROHM LINE – OPTIC TRENCH & OBLIQUE TRENCH, a line running S.W. & N.E. just this side of HOLLEBEKE & touching up with	

Army Form C. 2118.

WAR DIARY
or
INTELLIGENCE SUMMARY.
(Erase heading not required.)

Vol. XII. Sept. 1916.

Place	Date	Hour	Summary of Events and Information	Remarks and references to Appendices
WYTSCHAETE	29		the 5th A. & S.H. on the left and the 35th Division on the right. At 6 P.M. orders were received for the Brigade to withdraw and for the Batt. its transfer in the area. O.10.C. & C. B.H.Q. was at MARTENS FARM & the 4 Coys. along the ZERO HOUSE ROAD. Unfortunately orders were mislaid B'Coy & they never failed to find it. Eventually an officer was sent, who found it & brought it out to camp at 2 P.M. on 30th Sept. The Coys. were bivouaced in wet stubble and long grass & in the rain spent a miserable night.	
	30		Rain fell all day & from the men had a bad time efforts were made & a hot meal & a rum ration were provided. A good deal of corrugated iron was found and 16 waterproof sheets. the men were made comfortable. Rifles and S.A.A. & L. Guns were cleaned & Casualty Ret. Strength Return	II / III

Nelson W. Carter Lt.Col.
1/10/16 Cmndg 1/6 H.S. Borderers

1/5th K.O.S.B. OPERATION ORDER No 10

Copy No. 10

Vol XVI Appendix I

Key map
WYTSCHAETE
1/10,000

1. Information has been obtained, pointing to the probability of the enemy withdrawing in the near future from his present front, to positions beyond the MESSINES-WYTSCHAETE Ridge or still further EAST.

The day on which the withdrawal will commence will be known as J DAY.

The boundaries of the Battalion and objective line in case of advance are shewn on Map X.

2. Careful watch must be obtained by the troops in the line for any signs of withdrawal on J Day.

If the enemy is seen to be retiring by day the Battalion in the line, 5th Q.S.H. on the Right, 5th K.O.S.B. on the Left will advance and occupy successively, the 3 lines shewn on Map X; but no advance will be made the 2nd line, if there is no prospect of reaching the 3rd line before Dark.

No advance will be made beyond the first line without orders from B. H.Q.

It should be understood that the lines as shewn on Map X are merely intended to indicate general lines on which the chief tactical localities are to be made good.

FIRST OPERATION

3(a) By H hour on J Day OC "D" Coy will move all his men who occupied posts east of a line, just B of BOLLARTBEEK to point O.7.b.5.6 back to old FRENCH TRENCH

2nd Lt Cairns and 16 O.R will be ordered up

Army Form C. 2118.

WAR DIARY
or
INTELLIGENCE SUMMARY.

(Erase heading not required.)

Instructions regarding War Diaries and Intelligence Summaries are contained in F. S. Regs., Part II. and the Staff Manual respectively. Title pages will be prepared in manuscript.

Place	Date	Hour	Summary of Events and Information	Remarks and references to Appendices

Page 2

in the old FRENCH trench from the
Rly 0.7.d.05.65
~~above~~ line, to the junction with the 14th Division
(14 A & S.H.) ready to advance with them.
He will be supported by another Platoon
of 'D' Coy disposed in the same line.

The Platoon occupying the 3 Posts
from PIMPERNEL to the above line will be
formed up in their present line, ready to advance
as soon as the barrage lifts.

36   There will be a barrage in front of the OLD
FRENCH LINE from the Railway on the Right
extending along the front of the 14th Division.

(c)   There will also be a barrage from Point O.7.b.3.6
to the Railway at O.7.b.7.9. The barrage in
front of the 14th Division will lift according to
time table and 2nd Lt. CAIRNS will advance
followed by support platoon at distance of 300x
behind it with the 14th A.& S.H. and will
co-operate with them by attacking PICCADILLY
FARM from the South.
                There is a large dugout here
capable of holding 100 men.

When this barrage comes level with
the barrage at Point O.7.b.7.9. this second
barrage will advance with it. The Platoon
in the 3 right posts of D Coy will advance
behind it and mop up the enemy position at
about O.7.b.65.85. This platoon will
then cover the Right flank of 2nd Lt CAIRNS
Platoon.
                It will be careful to avoid coming
under of barrage in the BOIS QUARANTE.
(d) After the Capture of PICCADILLY FARM 2nd Lt
CAIRNS will take up a position on the Ridge
immediately S.E of it.

Army Form C. 2118.

WAR DIARY
or
INTELLIGENCE SUMMARY.
(Erase heading not required.)

Instructions regarding War Diaries and Intelligence Summaries are contained in F. S. Regs., Part II. and the Staff Manual respectively. Title pages will be prepared in manuscript.

Place	Date	Hour	Summary of Events and Information	Remarks and references to Appendices

Page 3

(C) O.C. "B" Coy will advance ready to occupy successively the positions vacated by "D" Coy. sending 1 Platoon forward to occupy the present right posts held by "D" Coy. and one Platoon to follow up and occupy the Ridge from about O.7.b 5.8. to O.1.D.9.1. and 1 Platoon to occupy a position in OLD FRENCH LINE in Support.

4. If the enemy is seen retiring or if a blue smoke grenade signals are put up by the 5th A & S.H from the Crater about N.18.b.5.8. O.C. "C" Coy (Capt Gilmour) will give the signal for the advance of the Battalion by firing a blue smoke grenade from PIMPERNEL.

He will at the same time advise by runner Bn Hd Qrs. that he has done so. He will have a message written out, ready with only the time of departure to be put on it.

At the same time "C" Coy will send out a patrol of 1 Platoon (2nd Lt. ORR and 1½ Platoon) supported by another Platoon to N.E. end of BOIS QUARANTE at about O.7.b.8.3 to secure the E side of the Wood. He will also send out a small patrol of 1 L.G. sub-section and 1 Rifle section and a good N.C.O. to keep touch with the 5th A. & S.H. on the Right.

5. As "C" Coy quits its line, so "A" Coy will occupy and if necessary hold the Position vacated by "C" Coy.

When the smoke signals go up the Platoon of "A" Coy will occupy successively the OLD TRENCH LINE in which "C" Coy Hd Qrs are presently situated and then the front line trench.

Each Coy Commander as he moves will report to Bn H.Qrs.

Army Form C. 2118.

WAR DIARY
or
INTELLIGENCE SUMMARY.

(*Erase heading not required.*)

Instructions regarding War Diaries and Intelligence Summaries are contained in F. S. Regs., Part II. and the Staff Manual respectively. Title pages will be prepared in manuscript.

Place	Date	Hour	Summary of Events and Information	Remarks and references to Appendices

6. If no withdrawal takes place by day strong Patrols will be pushed out to the tactical localities at 7.30 p.m. as above and will be followed by the remainder of the Infantry of the Battalion in the line, as each successive line is made good by the Patrols.

~~The second line will be occupied as a defensive position and no further advance will be made until daylight.~~

7. (I) If the advance is made by day the Artillery will cover the advance, keeping known centres of Resistance under fire as long as possible.

II By night, the Artillery will "Stand to" ready to cover the advance of each patrol by a creeping barrage forming a "box" beyond the tactical objective of each patrol.

They will not open fire, unless called upon, by the Bn Commander concerned, through Bde H Qrs.

8. The advance of the Infantry should be made in depth, preferably in small columns and platoons and sections should be specially detailed to deal with every known or suspected M.G. emplacement or Pill-Box.

II Every unit must be responsible for the safety of its own flanks, using its supports and reserves for the purpose, instead of dropping troops from the leading echelons, in any case, however, flank patrols must be detailed to gain and keep touch with the Divisions on the Right and Left, especially on the Right.

III If opposition is met with reserves must be pushed in at the weak spots, and not to reinforce troops held up.

Army Form C. 2118.

WAR DIARY
or
INTELLIGENCE SUMMARY.

(Erase heading not required.)

Instructions regarding War Diaries and Intelligence Summaries are contained in F. S. Regs., Part II. and the Staff Manual respectively. Title pages will be prepared in manuscript.

Place	Date	Hour	Summary of Events and Information	Remarks and references to Appendices

5 Kings own Scottish Borderers

Casualty List

Vol XLI Appendix II

First Phase:-

	Officers	O.R's
Killed	-	8
Wounded	2×	37
Missing	-	-
Total	2	45

Second Phase

	Officers	O.R's
Killed	1⊙	4
Wounded	1†	59
Missing	-	2
	2	65

× Lieut. IAN McHARDY
   2 Lieut. LFA EDGELL } 3rd /KOSB
⊙ 2 Lieut J. Alston   5th HLI
†   "   O.T. ROXBURGH   5 KOSB

Vol XLI Appendix III

1/5 Bn Kingown Scottish Borderers

Appendix No ———— to War Diary for Month of September 18

	Ofrs	ORs
(1) Strength at 31-8-18	41	727

		Ofrs	ORs
(2) Casualties:-	Killed	1	12
	Wounded	3	96
	Missing	—	2
		4	110

	Ofrs	ORs
(3) Transfers &c:-	4	4

	Ofrs	ORs
(4) Reinforcements	8	80

	Ofrs	ORs
(5) Strength at 30-9-18	41	750

Addendum to Para.6.

6(a)

(I). By day, no general advance will be made beyond the 1st (BLUE) line, without orders from Bde. H.Q., but patrols will be sent forward, if, and when the enemy is seen to be retiring from the 2nd (GREEN) line, i.e. the main WYTSCHAETE RIDGE. If orders are issued for a general advance to the 2nd (GREEN) line, no advance, except by patrols, is to be made to the 3rd (BROWN) line, if it is clearly impossible to reach and consolidate it before dark.

(II). By night, no general advance is to be made beyond the 1st line without orders from Bde. H.Q. Patrols will, however, be pushed out from this line, to keep touch with the enemy.

Addendum to Bn. Order. No. 10.

First Operation

O.C. "D" Coy. will have all his men moved clear of the area specified by 4:30 a.m. to-morrow. Whether the enemy is there or not, 2/Lt CAIRNS advances from OLD FRENCH LINE towards barrage line at H-5 minutes. Barrage comes down + H-5 minutes and lifts at H Hour, thereafter it advances by 100 yds. bounds every 3 mins, and extends to a line running W + N.E. when the road crosses. Rly. 8.a.7.1.

NOTE.
Para 3(a) last para commencing "It will be careful & Etc is cancelled. The barrage will have lifted by the time this platoon gets there. If it can seize the end of the Wood, it should do so, reporting position.

4(a) Advantage will be taken of the smoke + Barrage, + Capt. Gilmour, will push out his patrol as in 4, at H + 10 mins. at the same time putting up the blue smoke signal.

NOTE. This platoon will work with the rif section as scouts in front and its flanks protected by its Lewis Guns. When it has got forward 300 yards, it will be followed by its supporting platoon in similar formation. The supporting platoon will not leave the trench until the front platoon gained its distance.

Bearing of front platoon - from PIMPERNE 126° MAG: to N.E. corner of BOIS QUARANTE.

When patrols of C + D Coys reach the 1st BLUE line objective they will put up, as a signal, a single white Very light.

2

(a) Contact Aeroplanes will be marked by 2 black rectangular flaps attached to wires projecting from the lower plane on each side of the fuselage, and a trailing streamer on the rudder.

(b) They will call for signals by sounding the Claxon horn. If this is not answered they will drop a white light.

Flares when used, should be lit in groups of 3.

S. Day will be Sept 28th.

H. Hour will be notified later.

Every opportunity of making good the Blue line during the day will be taken. Any part of the Blue line not established during the day must be established as soon as possible after 7.30 p.m.

By Day.

If the enemy is seen retiring from the WYTSCHAETE RIDGE (green line) patrols must follow - a keep touch, and reports must be sent to the effect that they have started. A Patrol (1 Platoon) must be adequately supported by another Platoon, but no general advance will be made until orders from Bn. H. Qrs.

By Night.

Patrols must be pushed forward from the BLUE line to the GREEN line at 7.30 p.m. If this information indicates that the enemy has retired or is retiring from that line, a general advance will be commenced at that time.

The GREEN LINE if reached is to be consolidated as a defensive position, no further advance is to be made from it until ordered.

A block supplies line must be established. But if it will patrols pushed forward to keep touch with the enemy.

3

Bn. H.Q. will close at present position at present location at 8.30 p.m. and reopen at D. Coy. present H.Q. at same hour.

Prisoners of War will be sent to Bde. H.Q. under escorts not exceeding 10% guard.

Prisoners of War are not to be used as stretcher bearers more than once.

Officers are reminded that regular information is as good as position.

L 16/50 N points will troops in life.

The life of the day will be passing in front of the British divisions attacking from the lines. The line in the life for the troops doing is the same — Crimson line at PICCADILLY FARM, WHITE CHATEAU, but the canal bank about Bow Bridge. O.C. A & B. reporting at once that it has done so.

2. Communications

Coys. will have no signallers with them, but it is intended to form B/Hdrs. report centres at N.W. side of BOIS QUARANTE about O.4.b. central. at crossings of railway and roads at about O.8.b.6.1. and on the road immediately north of DOME HOUSE at about O.8.b.6.0. All reports should be sent by runner to these points, after crossing the first YELLOW LINE.

Capt.

Signals:—

Following rifle grenade signals will be used by patrols
RED Smoke means Held up by the enemy
BLUE do " Have reached second GREEN LINE.

In this way the centre of resistance will be outflanked.

(vii) Direction especially at night must be carefully kept and the leading patrols must be furnished with rough maps showing the landmarks, tactical localities and compass bearings to them and they must be provided with compasses.

(viii) Whenever a halt is made on the different objectives patrols must be pushed well to the front to keep touch with the enemy. Particularly at night these patrols must also be told that in front of the Second and Third lines they may possibly get in touch with British troops of the 41st Division advancing from the North West towards HOUTHEM

9. The 53rd Squadron R.A.F. have arranged for a contact patrol to be sent out at regular intervals should the advance take place all troops will be warned to indicate the positions when the contact patrol calls for them preferably by means of flares.

The 53rd Sqdn is also arranging to send out counter attack patrols at regular intervals to watch the front for any movement indicating a withdrawal.

10. Artillery. A barrage table is attached. Battery 152 Bde. 18 pdrs. will cover the advance of the Bn and a liaison artillery officer will be at Bn. H.Q. Coy Commanders should report to Bn. HQrs at once if they require support giving co-ordinates of area they wish shelled. The enemy has direct observation fire on SHEPE and WYTSCHAETE village so 19. Runners must avoid this area. 4.6" Hows. will

11. Machine Guns. 4 guns will cover the advance of the Bn. One section (4 guns) will cover the right flank of the Bn under the direct orders of M.G. Battn.

6.

1 section under 2/Lt Macready will be under the direct orders of the C.O. Liaison officer at Bn HQ. 2nd Lt Abernethy, who will transmit orders to sub sections "A" & "B" Coys will each have a party of 10 men at 8 pm on J-1 day at their own Coy HQ. 2nd Lt Roberts will send for A Coy party & 2nd Lt Macready for B Coy party. On J-1 day rations will be drawn for both parties by the M.G. Coy from Q.M. 5th KOSB. Water will also be provided.

12. <u>Light Trench Mortars</u>
   2 Stokes Guns under 2nd Lt Petty will be attached to the Bn and will be known as the left forward section. The Guns will be at SNIPERS BARN O.1.C.30.4.
   On J-1 day at 8 pm A & B Coys will each send a party of 4 men to report to 2nd Lt Petty at this point. The L.T.M.B. will draw rations on J-1 day from Q.M. 5th KOSB.

13. <u>Clothing Equipment.</u>
   (a) Fighting kit as usual will be worn except that greatcoats will be carried in place of water proof sheets, rolled over the top of haversacks and fastened on.
   (b) Every man in the platoons will carry one tin of flares and one disc for signalling to Aircraft. Each Coy and Platoon HQ will carry not less than 2 S.O.S. Grenades.
   Each rifle section will carry 3 cup attachments for No 23 grenade or 3 Grenade Dischargers for No 36 rifle grenade discharger.

V

Every man in the Rifle Sections will carry 2 No 23 or 21 Grenades according to which of the above is carried

(c) Each man will carry one complete days ration on "J" day in addition to unexpired portion of same days ration. Also an emergency ration in addition. The emergency ration must be made up by J day without fail. All men except those specially exempted will carry 170 rds SAA. The additional bandolier will be carried on the top of the haversack with the string sticking out. Reserve Ammunition can only be obtained from Bde and strict fire control is therefore necessary.

14. H hour and "J" day will be notified later. All preparations will be completed by the evening of the 26 Sept.

Units will be in readiness to move from H hour J day.

15. One Platoon of Cyclists will be attached to the Bde from noon 24th Sept.

One Section will be attached to each Bn for special patrol work and should <u>not</u> be used for despatch carrying.

16. Arrangements will be made by Bns in the line for patrols to signal the fact that they have reached the Second (GREEN) line, using the following signal Rifle Grenades :-

(a) By day ——— "RED Smoke"
(b) By night ——— WHITE and WHITE and WHITE

- 8 -

Patrols will also signal when they are held up by the enemy using a "BLUE" smoke Rifle Grenade signal. Arrangements are being made for Bn. in the line to receive a supply of each of the above to enable Platoons to have 2 of each.

17. 2nd Bn. Hdrs. today will be at C7.c.0.8 (present Left front Coy HQ) then as:—

	Column A	Column B
Order Brigade HQ	N.10.b.2.7	N.18.b.05.90
Right Bn. HQ	N.18.b.55.85	B
Left	C.1.C.0.8	B
Reserve	N.11.a.8.4	B
LTM Bty	N.10.b.2.7	N.18.b.05.90
B Coy MGC	N.10.b.2.7	N.18.b.05.90
C Coy MGC	YORKE HOUSE	B
Left Artillery Gp	H.32.8.6.8	N.3.a.3.3

(Note. B= somewhere in captured territory)

No further move forward of Headquarters will take place until after the capture of WYSCHAETE Second objective. Headquarters will then move into position shown in Column B above.

18. Regimental Aid Post.
   Position will be notified later.

19. 2nd Lt Gillespie is detailed as Liaison officer with 42nd Bgde. He will report at this HQ at H.28.d.5.1. at 6 pm on J—1 day.

20. ACKNOWLEDGE.

Captain
a/Adjt 15/R.I.R.

Army Form W. 3121.

Date of Recommendation.

Corps.

Division.

Brigade.

Schedule No. (to be left blank)	Unit	Regtl. No.	Rank and Name (Christian names must be stated)	Action for which commended (Date and place of action must be stated)	Recommended by	Honour or Reward	(To be left blank)

Copy No. 10

ADMINISTRATIVE ORDERS

1. Supplies

The system of supply will be as follows:-
On S-2 day there will be double refilling.
Rations for consumption on S-1 and S Day are to be sent up to the Units on the night of S-2/S-1. The ration situation at noon on S-1 day will then be as follows:-

On the man - rations for consumption S-1 Day & 1 Day (plus 1 Iron Ration)

At Transport lines - rations for consumption S+1 Day

2. Lt. .... Boyes has been detailed to take charge of the animals. This officer will report to .... F.O. at the Relay Transport lines at S-1 ...

3. Battery Kit

Surplus kit should be .... to .... by .... & .... at the Camp rather than on that night.

Copy No. 1 ....
        2 ....
        3 ....
        4 ....
        5 ....
        6 .... in Command
        7 ....

                Captain
            .... R.A. S.C.

Army Form C. 2118.

WAR DIARY
or
INTELLIGENCE SUMMARY.
(Erase heading not required.)

Instructions regarding War Diaries and Intelligence Summaries are contained in F. S. Regs., Part II. and the Staff Manual respectively. Title pages will be prepared in manuscript.

Place	Date	Hour	Summary of Events and Information	Remarks and references to Appendices

14. W.
16 sheets

1/5 K038
7856

Loan Diary
of
Kung Oun Neethah Bardoa
₹ 31/10/18

Vol IX — II

Mor-1806-31/10/05

WAR DIARY or INTELLIGENCE SUMMARY

Army Form C. 2118.

Vol. XLII   1st Oct. 1916

Place	Date	Hour	Summary of Events and Information	Remarks and references to Appendices
ZANVOORDE	1.		Bn. marched at 06:00 to ST. ELOI & LOCK No. 5 to P.2.E.9.0 just west of ZANVOORDE. The roads were in an appalling condition. Lewis guns had to be manhandled 2½ miles before the limbers were reached. The men stood the march well as muddy roads congested with traffic was very felt out. The day was fine & equipment was tried up. The bivouac area was long grass and stubbles and on the whole fairly good. A cold wind was blowing but the men seemed to take my plan. Bivi fell at night.	
	2	07:30 am	Orders came from Brigade to be ready to move at one & the C.O. went to Bde H.Q. the Bn. marched at 11 A.M. to P.5.C.6.4. C.O. & Coy Commanders reconnoitred for a position and became to Bdes 8th N.S.R. and 5th A.& S.H. being detailed to relieve a Bn. of the 35th Division. Eventually "A" Coy. went to BEGNAEKT TARM. C & B Coy. taking up a position on the front of the	

Army Form C. 2118.

WAR DIARY
INTELLIGENCE SUMMARY.
(Erase heading not required.)

Vol XLII. Oct. 1915.

Place	Date	Hour	Summary of Events and Information	Remarks and references to Appendices
WERVICQ	3.		A quiet day with a bright autumn sun. The men brightened up considerably. Communication in the wood improved. "A" Coy. proceeded after dusk to a wood in A.7.a.7.7 in reserve to 5th A.&S.H. Field kitchen shelled with 4.2 and 77mm H.E. 1 casualty.	
	4.		The wood was shelled with 4.2 and 77mm. H.E. 2 killed 3 wounded	
	5.		"A" Coy. returned to its bivouac area in the wood on ceasing to act as reserve to 5th A.&S.H. The wood was again shelled	
	6.		Bn. moved at 18.30 to bivouac area in J.35.	
	7.		Coy. training and training of specialists.	
	8.		2/Lt. CAIRNS to hospital. Coy. training and training of specialists. MAJOR G.R.S. PATERSON M.C. 2nd in command. LT. R.J. RICHARDSON to hospital.	
	9.		Coy. training. Battn. provided working-parties for construction of new support line.	
	10.		Coy. training. Working-parties again provided at night for work on new support line. 2/Lt. R.B. ORR wounded.	

WAR DIARY

Place	Date	Hour	Summary of Events and Information	Remarks and references to Appendices
	11		Orders received for the Division to continue the advance. C.O. commanded to company commanders the verbal orders received from Brigade.	
	12		Batt'n relieved two companies Royal North Lancs and two companies Queens (on 7th) in the line in K.33. "B" Coy in old line with all 16 posts N.E. of the YPRES MENIN ROAD; A Coy in support; "C" Coy and "D" Coy in reserve Bn H.Q. in K.31.c.9.7. Enemy counter preparation bombardment of our front and support lines with gas and H.E. 2/Lt. Barnsfather and 2/Lt. Corrie wounded, also 7.O.R.s.	
	13	19.00	H.Q. moved to forward positions in Q.3. & 3.2. Major G.R.S. PATTERSON M.C. M.L.I. now in command, Colonel R.N. Coulson proceeding on leave to U.K. 2/Lt. J. KIRK. Assembly positions were marked out by tape in front of the posts and clear of the Enemy's barrage zone. Companies occupied there positions by 0200 onwards Capt. D. GILMOUR wounded.	
	14	03.00	Enemy bombardment on our area with H.E. gas and smoke shells. Our bombardment commenced at 05.32 according to time table. Infantry advanced at 05.35, 'B' Coy in front, 'A' in support inclining to the right to come finally into the line with 'B' Coy. 'D' in reserve and 'C' behind to meet up GHELUWE from the North. The morning was very misty, and this combined with the smoke barrage from our own barrage and what from the enemy's screen made it impossible to see for more than 5 yards. Officers marched on compass bearing and the Scout Sergeant with three scouts marched on the left of 'B' Coy with compass for two hours it was impossible to maintain touch with other units however close. Progress began to come in about 06.30 the enemy accounted much and the only opposition encountered was from M.G.s in Pill-boxes	

WAR DIARY

Place	Date	Time	Summary of Events	Remarks and references to Appendices
	14		The first objective (black line) was early reached and by 08.00 small parties were pushing on the second objective (blue line). Strong opposition was met here from UNIFORM FARM (R.I.C.7.7.) where 1 Hy. Gy, 1 trench mortar and 3 7.77 mm guns were turned simultaneously on our troops. The field guns firing with open sights at a range of 500°. Capt. BROWN.C. D Coy was killed. Lt. HOOD pushed forward with a handful of men, rushed the farm, chasing over thirty of the enemy from it and captured the three guns. About 09.00 the mist began to clear and it was possible to see around. He then discovered that apart from the six men he had with him, there were no more of our troops in sight. He therefore withdrew to Q.6. central to seam to form told off the pill box and farm buildings there. More men began to arrive, and at mid-day 'C' Coy. moved forward to recapture UNIFORM FARM which had meantime been occupied by the enemy gunners. Lt. J. M.T. DICKIE with Sgt. GALLACHER and 4 men crept forward under the fire of the guns and again reached the farm. 33 of the enemy ranfrom it. The farm was in our hand by 12.50, and the second objective completely secured by 13.15. Meanwhile Bn. H.Q. had moved to Auckin farm the line was consolidated and the 5th A.S.H. passed through to the final objective (brown line). Days spent in consolidation of a different line and gathering of salvage. The bodies of 2Lt. KIRK and 8 men were removed & buried in Q.3.8.3.2	
	15	18.00	Battn. occupied SNOOKER FM.(A), RUMANIAN FM.(B). VAN AKKERS 17 FM.(C) and UNIFORM FARM (D). Battn H.Q. moved to Q.6. central.	

WAR DIARY

PLACE	DATE	TIME	Summary of Events and Information	Remarks and reference to appendices
	16th		Captured guns were collected amounting to 5. 77mm and 3. 4.2 Howitzer 18.30. Battn. took up the line of the railway from LIMBER FM to R.8 & 7.2 Battn. H.Q. the RUMANIAN FM.	
	17th		Colonel F.J. COURTENAY HOOD D.S.O. took command of the Battalion "C" Coy. moved to RIPE FM. "D" the FURMACLIN FM, but orders were then received for the Battn. to concentrate in the area R.4. "A" Coy. moved to PARAGON FM. B.C. and D. to RAINBOW FM, Bn H.Q. to RAISIN H.Q.	
	18th		All men in the Battn. were given a hot bath Billets were cleaned Orders received to be ready to move forward.	
	19th		Battn. marched to LAVWE, billeting area in R21a. The men were in excellent spirits, the band marched at the head of the Battn. The civilians - just liberated - extended a hearty welcome to British troops.	
	20th	1000	Divine Service. Remainder of day spent cleaning equipment & billets	
	21st		Coy. & Specialist training	
	22nd		" " "	
	23rd		A & B Coys. on 30 yds Rifle Range C. & D. Coys on Specialist training. C. & D. Coys on 30 yds Rifle Range Brigade order received to the effect that the Brigade would move to area about N.36.c.9.d.	

WAR DIARY.

Place	Date	Hour	Summary of Events and Information	Remarks and references to Appendices
	24th	08.00	Battalion paraded, ready to move.	
		09.00	Battalion moved off to Area about N.36.c.&d. VIA main AELBEKE Rd. ROLLEGHEM - BELLEGHEM.	
		13.00	Midday meal on road about 7.5.d.	
		15.00	Moved off to Area N.36.c.&d. Battalion HdQrs established at N.36.d.5.3	
		16.50	Orders received. 1/5th K.L.13. would be placed at the disposal of 102nd Inf. Bde. 1 Officer attached to 102 Inf. Bde. HdQrs.	
	25th	07.00	Rifle and billet Inspection. Battalion ready to move.	
		10.30	16 coy. 1/5th K.L.13. sent off to be attached to 1/7th Yorkshire.	
		14.30	Orders received for 1/5th K.L.13. to move forward to position of readiness about U.3.a.C.&d.	
		16.15	Battalion moved off.	
		19.00	Battalion Billited as follows:- Batn HdQrs at U.3.c.&9.7. A coy at U.3.a.7.2. B coy at U.3.a.7.1. C coy at U.3.a.9.4. D coy with Yorkshire at U.11.b.8.9.	
		21.00	Orders recd. for 1 Officer per coy to reconnoitre crossing at U.6.c.4.9. & U.16.c.1.9.	
		24.15	Above order cancelled. Brigade order received to the effect that 1/5th K.L.13. would now come under orders of 103rd Inf. Bde. and would move on 26th inst. to ST. ANNE Area. (N.19.)	
	26th	09.30	Battalion Parade.	

WAR DIARY

Date	Hour	Summary of Events and Information	Remarks and references to appendices
26/10/1918	0700	Battalion ready to move off. Head of column at "starting point" X roads, U.2.6.	
	1015	Battalion moved off. Route by road through U.1.6 - N.36.d. - main road at N.36.d. - LE CHAT CAB. - BEUEGHEM. KLIJTTGAT. SIANNE.	
	14.30	Battalion H.Q.rs established at N.14.C.1.0. Coys billeted in Koyoe in N.19.b.d.	
	22.00	Brigade order received. Brigade would move to DESSELGHEM Area (C.14.d.)	
27/10/1918	07.30	Billets cleaned out and battalion ready to move	Ref. map sheet 29.N.W.
	10.00	Battalion moved off. Route via COUTRAI - STRACEGHEM - HARLEBEKE to SPRIETE	
	12.30	Brigade formed up in area about H.6.d. L.b. for midday meal.	
	13.45	Battalion moved off.	
	17.00	Battalion H.Q.rs established at SPRIETE about C.21.d.2.6. Companies billeted in farms near cross roads.	
	20.00	Orders received to the effect that 103rd Bde moved jellew 1010 Rifles on the line 25 mins' behind Pan Bay more ser. Off. to reconnitr. route to line.	
28/10/1918	1.00	I appui Pan Bay more ser. Off. to reconnitr. route to line.	Ref. map sheet 29.I. N.E.
	15:30	Battalion moved off. Route from STRIETE VIA 897 central - J.10.c.3.7. BELGEIK - VICHTE - VOSSENHOEK.	
	18.30	Battn. H.Q. established at J.2.6.d.8.8.	
	23.00	Relief complete. Coys H.Qrs established as follows: A coy - P.4.b.0.8. B coy J.34.a.9.5. b coy J.27.d.9.9. D coy J.28.d.1.5. During the night a gap of nearly 1000 yds. was left to our left. A patrol of D coy from line posts were advanced to conform to the R.2.F. line on our left. Astrew during the night from farm in J.35.a. bint-owing to the spread the enemy to withdraw during the night from farm in J.35.a. position taken up by the enemy V.E. of farm. The farm was rendered unternable and our party withdrew.	
29/10/1918	06.00	Outs. zone line was our line running (approx) - P.4.B.3.0. - P.4.b.8.0. - J.34.d.56.	

WAR DIARY.

Place	Date	Hour	Summary of Events and Information	Remarks and references to Appendices

J.29.c.9. – J.29.c.9.7.1. During the day the enemy Artillery was Active on roads in our rear. Aero. Operations active. Noises and preparations made for advance which was to take place in the morning of 31st inst.

30th 21:30 British closed at J.26.a.8.5.1 required some time at STERHOEK J.28.d.9.2
31st 02:00 10 French Tanks and 1 Coy A.M.H. attached to Battn. to assist in advance.
      06:00 Coys were in position or jumping off line which ran from J.29.c.2.6. South to J.36.a.2.1.
            There is J.35.a.6.0. Approx.
      08:25' Our ARTILLERY opened down barrage 300 yds in front of jumping off line lying at the rate of 100yds in 3 minutes. Our M.G. put down barrage for 20 minutes on a line running N.& S. from J.29.a.8.0. to J.35.a.2.0. Simultaneously our Infantry moved forward. 1 section to accompany each tank was provided by A Coy. Immediately and barrage opened the Enemy put down the barrage 100 was jumping off line. In spite of strong opposition met with on enemy jump' line posts the tanks and Infantry reached objective forward mopping up enemy posts capturing Br. Gs. and many prisoners. The thick fog and smoke promote a splendid action for our advancing infantry.
      06:15' Our Infantry had reached the firsts objective which was a line running J.30.c.7.3. South to J.36.c.5.
           A M.G. Coy with 4 tanks in vicinity of farm at J.36.c.4.6
           B & C Coys holding a line from farm at J.36.a.4.3 north to railway.
           4 Tanks under Capt A. Patton J.36.a.4.3
      08:30 All Coys with 8 tanks moved forward, having got in touch with 310th Div. on right and L.T.B. on left.
      08:35' Our Artillery barrage opened on 310th Bn. and 410th Div. fronts. Our Infantry and Tanks, being close up to the barrage line, pushed on a line K.25.c.5.0.

WAR DIARY.

Place	Date	Hour	Summary of Events and Information	Remarks and references to appendices
	31.		to K.31.a.5.3. till the barrage lifted, then pushed forward in direction of BALGIE CABT.	
		10-45	A.Coy. with remnants of B.& D.Coys, had reached final objective road — holding positions on railway in K.32.a. & road cuttings K.32.a.0.5 & K.31.b.9.4. In the mopping up of houses in K.31.b.6., eight few prisoners were taken, the enemy having withdrawn to high ground about K.26.central. During the remainder of the day, heavy M.G. & T.M. fire was experienced from farms & homes about K.26. Central. One enemy 77mm. gun about church in GYSELBLEOHTEGHEM was very active during the day.	
		14-30	Orders were issued for a further advance to be made. The 5th K.O.S.B. were to push forward & establish themselves along road running from cross roads in K.32.b. south, to railway, while the 5th A.& S.H. on left would take up a line from cross roads in K.26.a. to cross roads in K.32.b. south to railway, while the 5th A.& S.H. on left would take up a line from cross roads in K.26.a. to cross roads in K.32.b.	
		14-45	6 tanks attempted to clear farms & houses about K.26 central, but owing to heavy fire from 4, M.G.s & the enemy 77mm gun in vicinity of church, were forced to withdraw. 2 tanks were put out of action with direct hits.	
		16-30	Above orders for further advance were cancelled.	
		21-00	Orders were issued to the effect that A.& B Coys would push strong patrols forward & if possible, establish line on road running from cross roads in K.32.b. to railway while 5th A.& S.H. moved forward to take up line on road from cross Rds in K.32.b. to cross roads in K.26.a.	

War DIARY

Summary of Events and Information

PLACE	DATE	TIME		Remarks and references to appendices
	3105	2300	Our patrols moved forward. Enemy had evacuated high ground North of railway. The new line had been established with A. Coy on left, B Coy on right. B & D Coys holding position on railway line and road leading to K.32.c.	
		2400	Touch had been gained with A&B H on left, and B Coy had established liaison posn. 6" of railway, in touch with 3105 Bn.	
		2445	A patrol from A. Coy was reported to have reached a point about K.3.3.2.a.9. without having encountered the enemy. During the whole day operations communication was good, in spite of heavy fog in the earlier part of the day and smoke being sent up by shell fire. Companies were always in touch with each other and Battalion Headquarters kept informed as to the progress and situation of companies by runners. During the day our casualties amounted to 15 killed and 48 wounded.	

H.H.White 2 Lieut
Bn. St officer

War Diary, October, 1918.

Appendix I.

Congratulatory Messages to the Battalion.

1.

[Copy of Wire.]

To All Companies

14th.

The Major-General sends his heartiest congratulations to the Battalion on their splendid performance to-day. A.A.A.

The B.G.C. cannot express his pleasure at the Battalion's performance. A.A.A.

The C.O. thanks all ranks for their splendid performance and is sure that, in spite of fatigue, to-morrow's deeds, should we be required, will be even greater than to-day's.

from G.R.S. PATERSON, M.C.
MAJOR,
cmdg. 1/5 th K.O.S.B.

2.

[Copy of Wire]

from WAGA
to LESA

14th, 20.00 hours.

The Divisional and Brigade commanders congratulate all ranks on the success gained to-day by their hard and determined fighting A.A.A. Prisoners up to date nearly 600, also 3 guns.

3.

[Copy of Wire.]

from WAGA
to LESA.

14K. 22.50 hours.

Message from army commander begins AAA
Please accept my congratulations and convey

3.

them to all commanders and troops engaged to-day on the very successful results in what has been a long and arduous day.

Appendix No. 1 to War Diary, October 1918.

		Ofrs.	O.R's.
1.	Strength at 30/9/18.	41	750
2.	Killed	3	32
	Wounded	6	154
	Missing	-	--
	Total	9	186
3.	Transfers, sick, Invalided, etc.	8	58
4.	Reinforcements	2	30
5.	Strength at 31/10/18.	26	536

1/5th King's Own Scottish Borderers.

Casualty List. 1/10/18 - 4/10/18.

	Officer	O.R.
Killed	3x	32
Wounded	6ø	154
Missing	-	-
Total	9.	186.

```
x,  2/Lieut. J.A.KIRK
    Capt. W.S.BROWN
    2/Lt. J.J.MUNRO
    ...........
ø   2/Lt. R.B.ORR
     "    F.R.CORRIE
     "    R.M.BAIRNSFATHER
    Capt. J.M.M.GILMOUR, M.C.
xxx
    2/Lt. W.GRAHAM
    Capt. W, MACDONALD.
```

1/5th King's Own Scottish Borderers.

	Officers.	O.Rs.
(1) Strength at 31st October, 1918.	26	536.
(2) Casualties { Killed	–	–
Wounded	–	–
Missing.	–	–
	–	–
(3.) Transfers, sick, Invalided, etc.	1	83.
(4). Reinforcements.	8	262
(5.) Strength at 30th November, 1918.	33	715.

CONFIDENTIAL

15-W.
21 sheets

988

WAR DIARY
of
1/5th King's Own Scottish Borderers. T.F.

From 1/11/18. To. 30/11/18.

VOLUME XLIII.

WAR DIARY
INTELLIGENCE SUMMARY
(Erase heading not required.)

Army Form C. 2118.

Place	Date	Hour	Summary of Events and Information	Remarks and references to Appendices
Map	1st May 1918	0500	"A" & "B" Coys 1/5th K.O.S.B. were moving from Railway at K.32.d.9.0. to Cross Roads at	
Sheet 29 N.E.			K.32.2. "B" Coy on right had liaison post S. of railway on right with 31st Div.	
1/20,000			"A" Coy on left were in touch with 5th A. & S.H. "C" & "D" Coys were holding positions	
			about Railway & road cutting in K.32.2. The Tanks had withdrawn to	
			Rear Areas.	
		0500	Our advance appears to have been established at home on Railway K.31.a.8.9.	(M)
			During the day Enemy artillery was quiet.	
		11.30	Orders were issued to the effect that A. & S.H. with taking over the line from Railway	
			at K.32.d.9.0. to Cross Roads in K.26.a. & 5th K.O.S.B. would concentrate to arrival	
			at STERHOEK on completion of relief	
		16.00	Reln. complete. Battalion H.Q. located at T.35.d.4.8. and proposed some time at	
			STERHOEK.	
		16.30	Line all limbered in firms and horses in wrecks of STERHOEK	
	2nd May	18.30	The day was spent cleaning equipment and billets.	
		11.30	Thought & Services	
		21.30	Brigade Orders received. Brigade make out 3rd post to BISSEGHEM. Posts to be taken over	

Army Form C. 2118.

WAR DIARY
or
INTELLIGENCE SUMMARY.
(Erase heading not required.)

Instructions regarding War Diaries and Intelligence Summaries are contained in F. S. Regs., Part II. and the Staff Manual respectively. Title pages will be prepared in manuscript.

Place	Date	Hour	Summary of Events and Information	Remarks and references to Appendices
			VICHTE — IN DE KIOK CAB^t — STEENBRUGGE — STACEGHEM — LUCK9 — COURTRAI — H.S Central — BISSEGHEM.	
R.I. Map	3rd/10/18	0800	Billets reconn^d and Billeting Pards in front 6/1	
Sh. 29 N.W.		0910	Battalion moved off.	
1/20,000		1045	Battalion passed bridge on the point — N.14.TC × RDS.	
		1300	Battalion arrived in Bivouac at E.9.6 & 8.0	
		14.15	A. & Q. moved off.	
		1700	H.Q. taken over Billets in house E. d BISSEGHEM. Men H.Q. re-established at B.15.d 2.1. Ranks also at the disposal of personnel and a	
			A.w. in Battalion to clean up kits and equipment. Ranks also at the disposal of personnel and a	
			Lim. Range of instruction also issued by the Bn.	
			C.O. Platoon were placed in Training Gun Range. Rifle Range.	
			Brigade Order received. Brigade would move to HOLLEBEKE & a.m.	
	4th/10/	2300	Above Order cancelled	
	5/10/		Day fixed in Specht. Training Gun Bayonet Rifle Range.	
	6/10/		Coy. fitted out Specht & Training. Brigade Order received. Brigade would move to	
	7/10/		BALDWIN Out. Sucket Road to Le Bahre - thence MENINTARE — MENIN — cross LYS via	

WAR DIARY
or
INTELLIGENCE SUMMARY.
(Erase heading not required.)

Army Form C. 2118.

Place	Date	Hour	Summary of Events and Information	Remarks and references to Appendices
	8th Nov	0900	MARATHON Bridge to HALLUIN. All men view of Billets and Billets cleared.	
		0945	Battn formed ready to move off.	
		0955	Battalion moved off.	
		1230	Brigade arrived in HALLUIN. 1/5th K.O.S. went to billets in two large factories.	
			A recreation room was fixed up near billets for the benefit of the men and arrangements were made for starting sports.	
	9th Nov	0900	The morning was devoted to Coy, Platoon and Specialist training.	
			Trips into town were held off to the 1st day, Hospital bills and recreation Room	
			The afternoon was devoted to games.	
	10th Nov	1100	Divine Service held in town Music Hall.	
			The afternoon was devoted to games.	
		0930	"Armistice had been signed" Handsome received. The Band immediately turned out and midst old hand shouts marched off through the town to the Grand Place followed by a happy crowd of men from the Battalion and other units in the Vicinity. The scene was lit up by flares put up by the R.A.F.	

WAR DIARY
INTELLIGENCE SUMMARY

Place	Date	Hour	Summary of Events and Information	Remarks and references to Appendices
	11th Nov	1100	After paying for some time in the Aerodrome ground the Band marched to Parade ½ [illeg] followed by the troops. See the also with had a speech from the General. The G.O.C's speech was received with great applause. After playing for some time from 11.15 (?) the Bandsmen marched back to their respective huts. Brigade Ceremonial parade. Officer's Church in Camp. Col. Hope took the command of 162nd Inf. Brig. Maj. Johnstone assumed command of 113th Inf. R.C.B	
	12th Nov		Hereof - Day Platoons and Specialist training. Afternoon devoted to games.	
	14th Nov	1000	Brigade Order received. Brigade will now move to DOTTIGNIES area on 14th Inst.	
		10.15	Have tea at billets at 9.Hrs reserved	
		1030	Bn Parade ready to move	
		1545	Bn marches off via BRUYELLE - ESTAIMPUIS - WARCOING - ESCANAFFLES - AMOUGIES - RUSSEIGNES - RONSE - ORROIR - HERENM - MOUSCRON - DOTTIGNIES.	
			Battalion arrived at DOTTIGNIES.	
			Immediately on arrival a hot meal was issued to the men	
		1930	Boys would march to Nouveau Prison 13th Bn	
	15th Nov	1700	Battn started from a and billets in up.	

WAR DIARY or INTELLIGENCE SUMMARY

Army Form C. 2118.

Place	Date	Hour	Summary of Events and Information	Remarks and references to Appendices
		1115	Battalion paraded ready to move off	
		1130	Battalion moved off. Route taken via Espierre – WARCOIN – HERRINES – MOLENBAIX	
		1630	Battalion arrived at MOLENBAIX. Battalion H.Q. and Transport billeted in Chateau. Coys. into Billets in b Mayor and farms in the vicinity	
4th Nov.		2000	Advance were received. Brigade would move to area near RENAIX on the 16th inst	
16th Nov.		0900	Billets cleaned & standard made of billets	
		0945	Battalion paraded ready to move off	
		1000	Battalion moved off. Route taken via – CELLS – BEAUREGARD – ANSEOEUL – WAYRIPONT – BIEGH – TER-STOCKE	
		1430	Battn. arrived TER STOCKE. Immediately on arrival new Coy. officers and where accompanied by billeting parties on bicycles proceeded in TER STOCKE	
17th Nov.		1000	Divine Service.	
		1100	Coys were warned to move to billets in RENAIX the afternoon. Div. details to proceed to Guards Brigade. On receipt of code Battn. proceeded with to Oe Nov 18th inst.	

Army Form C. 2118.

WAR DIARY
INTELLIGENCE SUMMARY.
(Erase heading not required.)

Instructions regarding War Diaries and Intelligence Summaries are contained in F. S. Regs., Part II. and the Staff Manual respectively. Title pages will be prepared in manuscript.

Place	Date	Hour	Summary of Events and Information	Remarks and references to Appendices
OGY	18 Nov	07.20	Billets cleared and Battalion paraded ready to move.	
		07.30	Battalion moved off	
		1000–1100	Route taken – ELLEZELLES – FLOBECQ – OGY.	
"			Battalion halted for an hour between ELLEZELLES and FLOBECQ, to allow another Brigade to pass through FLOBECQ.	
		1150.	Battalion arrived at OGY. Immediately on arrival, a midday meal was prepared for the men, and all coys. were comfortably billeted in the village. HQrs was established in the CHATEAU.	
"	19 Nov.		The morning was spent in cleaning up billets and overhauling equipment. The afternoon was devoted to games. A football match was played between "A" Coy. 1st K.O.S.B. and an Coy 5th A.S.H. Also the football match, live men from the same Batt. gave an exhibition boxing bout.	
"	20 Nov.		Lt. Col. Hook, D.S.O. assumed command of the Battalion	
		11.00	Battalion paraded for commanding Officer's inspection. The afternoon was devoted to games. A football match was played between D.Coy 5th K.O.S.B. and Brigade HQ. After the football match, two men of 5th K.O.S.B gave an exhibition boxing bout.	
"	21 Nov.	09.30.	Battalion Parade.	

Army Form C. 2118.

WAR DIARY
INTELLIGENCE SUMMARY.
(Erase heading not required.)

Instructions regarding War Diaries and Intelligence Summaries are contained in F. S. Regs., Part II. and the Staff Manual respectively. Title pages will be prepared in manuscript.

Place	Date	Hour	Summary of Events and Information	Remarks and references to Appendices
OCY.	21 Nov (Cont.)		Morning spent with Coy. Section and Reorganic drill.	
			Afternoon was devoted to games.	
			A bugle hunt was arranged and carried out in the afternoon, the dogs being borrowed from farmers in the vicinity.	
"	22 Nov	09.30.	Battalion parade for "smartening up" drill.	
		11.00.	Lecture by C.O. in village church on Educational and Demobilization Scheme.	
			The afternoon was devoted to games. A football match was played between our Coy. K.O.S.B. and our Coy. A.S.H. An exhibition Boxing Bout was put up by two representatives of the above Battalions during the interval.	
"	23 Nov	09.00	Coy. parades. Coy. Commanders lectured on Educational Scheme.	
		10.00.	Battalion Route march.	
			Afternoon was devoted to games. An Officers' football match was played at WANNEBEEQ between our Coy K.O.S.B. and our Coy A.S.H.	
		18.00.	Divisional concert in LECCINES.	
"	24 Nov	12.00	Divine Service on Battalion Parade Ground.	
			Afternoon – Platoon football matches were played.	

WAR DIARY
INTELLIGENCE SUMMARY.
(Erase heading not required.)

Army Form C. 2118.

Place	Date	Hour	Summary of Events and Information	Remarks and references to Appendices
OGY.	25 Nov	09.30	Battalion Parade. Ceremonial as "Smartening up" drill. Sorts were allotted to the Coys.	
		14.00	Afternoon devoted to sport. Platoon matches being played off.	
		16.00	Boxing class.	
"	26 Nov.	09.00	Battalion Parade. Ceremonial as "Smartening up" drill. Both were allotted to the Coys. and a clean change of clothing was issued to every man.	
		10.30	Coy. route marches, and practice in Advance Guards.	
			Afternoon was devoted to games. A Football match was played between one Coy. K.O.S.B. and one Coy. A.S.H.	
		14.00		
		16.30	Boxing class.	
"	27 Nov	09.30	Battalion Parade. "Smartening up" drill. "C" and "D" Coys. tactics — "A" and "B" Coys. route march. (advanced guards).	(N)
			Afternoon — games.	
"	28 Nov.	09.30	Battalion Parade. — ceremonial drill.	
			Afternoon — Final "Soccer" match — "D" Coy. K.O.S.B. v. "A" Coy. A.S.H. resulted in draw 1–1; decided to replay.	

Army Form C. 2118.

WAR DIARY
INTELLIGENCE SUMMARY.
(Erase heading not required.)

Instructions regarding War Diaries and Intelligence Summaries are contained in F. S. Regs., Part II. and the Staff Manual respectively. Title pages will be prepared in manuscript.

Place	Date	Hour	Summary of Events and Information	Remarks and references to Appendices
OGY.	29th Nov.	11.00	Inspection by B.G.C. 103rd Brigade at WANNEBECQ.	
"	30 Nov.		St Andrew's Day - Sports. Evening - Torchlight Procession.	

1/5th King's Own Scottish Borderers.
OPERATION ORDER No 22.   2-11-18

1. The 103rd Infantry Bde. Group will move to BISSEGHEM area to-morrow.

2. Units will march to Bde. Starting Point, X roads at VICHTE, I.94.d.8.4, by platoons at 100x intervals. Time of passing (1/5 KOSB) 1043.

3. Transport will join Battalion before passing Brigade Starting Point.
   Officers' mounts will be sent up at 08.30.

4. Battalion Starting Point will be Bn. H.Q. I.28.c.8.8., and Battalion will be formed up, with head of column at that point, remainder of column along road running S.E. through I.28.d.
   Order of march - H.Q., A, B, C, D.
   Coys. will be formed up in position (Coys at 100x intervals), ready to move off, by platoons, by 09.15 prompt. Bn. will move off with platoons at 100x intervals, but will close up to Coys. at 100x again, before passing Brigade Starting Point. Transport will observe usual distances.

5. Captain Crichton, 1. OR per Coy. and 1 from Bn. H.Q. will meet the Staff Captain at BISSEGHEM Church at 12 noon.

6. There will be a halt for a meal tomorrow between 12.30 and 13.30.

7. Route - VICHTE X roads - I.34.a - I.20.d - STACEGHEM - LOCK 9 - H.27.a.2.1 - Bridge in H.25.a - Bridge in BISSEGHEM.

2-11-18.

(Signed) R. Gillespie,
2/Lieut.
a/Adjt, 1/5 K.O.S.B.

1/5th K.O.S. Borderers.

Orders from Brigade have been received for Battalion to move on 3/11/18.

Reveille — 0600.
Breakfast — 0700.
Sick Parade — 0745.
L.G. Limbers & Horses for } — 0800.
Cookers &c. report
To be loaded at — 0830.
Officers Kits at Bn. H.Q. — 0800.
Mess Cart at Corps — 0815.
Batt⁻ⁿ clear of Billets — 0830.
Coy. Commanders responsible } — 0830.
for cleaning of billets by

Dress — Full Marching Order.
Tam 'o' Shanters to be worn.
Steel helmets and Jerkins on Packs, as before.

2-11-18

(Signed) K. Gillespie 2ⁿᵈ Lieut.
a/Adjt. 1/5 K.O.S.B.

1/5 K.O.S. Borderers.
AFTER ORDER
by
Lieutenant Colonel. F.J. Courtenay Hood DSO.
Commdg.   5-11-18.

1. The Brigade will move to new billeting area in vicinity of HALLUIN tomorrow, 6th inst. The Bn. Starting Point is the church, BISSEGHEM, the head of the Bde. column passing this point at 10.00.

2. The Bn. will form up in column of route opposite Bn. Orderly-Room at 09.30, in the following order:- H.Q., A, C, B, D. Coys. On moving off, the usual distance will be observed.
   The head of the column will pass Bde. Starting Point at 10.05.
   <u>Dress</u>:- Full marching order, wearing Tam-o'-Shanter. O/C. Coys. whose Coys. helmets are being painted, will ensure that proper precautions are taken to protect the helmets and clothing where the paint is not thoroughly dry.

3. <u>Reveille</u> 0600.
   <u>Breakfast</u> 0700.
   <u>Dinner</u> - On arrival in Billets.
   <u>Billets</u> - must be vacated, and ready for inspection by 09.00.

4. <u>Baggage Stores</u>:
   (a). Officers' Kits will be stacked at Q.M. Stores at 08.00.
   (b) Lewis Guns and equipment. O/C. Coys. will each detail their L.G. N.C.O. and 10 men to load these. The L.G.O. will superintend this, and the party will report to him at 08.00, at Transport Lines.
   (c). Baggage, ammunition, tools: O/C. Coys. will each detail 2 men to report to Q.M. as loading party, at 08.00.
   (d). Signalling Equipment. This will be loaded by 08.30, under supervision of Signalling Officer.
   (e). Q.M. will send guide to Bde. HQ at 08.30 to guide L.G. wagons with blankets for Bns. to Transport Lines.

5. <u>Advance Party</u>:
   2nd Lieut. W.G. Mattingley and the following personnel will report to the 2nd in Command at HALLUIN CHURCH at 10.00:-

Coy. Q.M.S. + Storeman.
N.C.O. from Bn.H.Q.
  "   "   I.O.
  "   "   Q.M.

Representatives from H.Q. Officers Mess and Coy mess. This party will report, ready to proceed, to the Adjutant, at 08.00.

5/11/18.

Signed. M Crichton, Capt.
 a/Adjt. 1/5" K.O.S.B.

WAR DIARY.

Battalion, King's Own Scottish Borderers.   Copy ...8...
        O P E R A T I O N   O R D E R . No.24.   13/11/18.

Reference Map Sheet 1/100,000 TOURNAI.

The 103rd Brigade will move via BECKEM - MOUSCRON - DOTTIGNIES to
DOTTIGNIES - WALGHEM Area tomorrow 14th Nov.

Move:- The Battalion will parade ready to march off at 10.00.
Starting Point Battalion Headquarters, order of march
Battalion Headquarters, B, C, D, A, Coys. transport. The following
distances will be maintained on the march 300 yards between
Battalions 100 yards between Coys. Every 6 vehicles 25 yards.

Dress:- Full marching Order, haversack ration will be carried on the
            man.

Advance Party:- 2/Lt. Gillespie, 2/Lt. Mattingley. 4 O.R.M.S's with
            Coy. Storemen. One N.C.O. Per Bn. H.Qts. transport,
and Q.M.Stores. will parade at 0700 At Battalion Headquarters. This
party will report to STAFF Capt. at Town Majors office, DOTTIGNIES
at 10.00 for instructions.

Transport:- Transport will accompany Battalion. L.G. Limbers will
                march in rear with Transport. Cookers will march
in rear of 1st Line Transport.
            Dinners will be served on arrival at new area.
            Mess Cart will report to Battalion Headquarters at 0730
            Maltise Cart will report to R.A.P. at 0730.

Baggage:- Blankets will be rolled in bundles of ten, labelled
              and stacked at Q.M.Stores by 0730. Officers Kits
will be dumped at Battalion Headquarters by 0730.

Instructions:- Police Cpl. and Police will report to Capt. Hood
                at rear of Battalion for duty.
                Billets will be left clean and tidy and a
                certificate rendered to Orderly Room.

Reports:- Battalion Headquarters until 10.00 Head of Column
              until arrival at new area.
              A marching out state will be handed to Adjutant by 0730.

            (Signed) A. MacBryde, Captain.
        Adjutant ---- King's Own Scottish Borderers.

Issued by Cyclist Orderly. 75.80.   13/11/18.

                    Distribution.

    Copy No.1......................................File.
      "   " 2......................................"A" Coy.
      "   " 3......................................B   "
      "   " 4......................................C   "
      "   " 5......................................D   "
      "   " 6......................................T.O.
      "   " 7......................................Q.M.
      "   " 8......................................War Diary.
      "   " 9......................................R.S.M.

War Diary

Battalion, King's Own Scottish Borderers.
Operation Order No.--
Ref. Map Sheet.--   14/11/1s.

The March East will be continued tomorrow.

MOVE.   The Battalion will move to the new area tomorrow. Battalion will parade at Zero ready to move of. Route as per Brigade Orders. Order of March, Headquarters, "C,D,A,B" Coys.
   Until further Orders. Coys. will take about as leading Coy. of Battalion. i,e, "C" Coy. tomorrow and so on on rotation.

DRESS.   Full Marching Order.

ADVANCE PARTY.   2/Lt. Gillespie, 2/Lt. Mattingley, 4 C.Q.M.S. with Coy. Storemen. One N.C.O. from Headquarters Coy. Transport, Q.M. store, will form permanant Advance Party for this Unit until further notice. Notification will be published daily of what hour above party will parade and destination.

TRANSPORT.   Will march with Battalion.
   L.Gun Limbers will accompany Transport.
   Cookers will march in rear of 1st. line Transport.
Mess Cart and Maltese Cart will report respectively to Battalion Headquarters and R.A.P. at Zero - 60.

BAGGAGE.   All blankets will be rolled labelled and dumped in bundles of ten at Q.M. Stores. before Breakfast.
   Officers valises etc. will be stacked at Q.M.Stores ready for loading at Zero - 90.
   Sgt.Mess Stores if any will be dumped at Q.M.Stores by Zero - 90.

INSTRUCTIONS.   Police Cpl. and Police will report daily to O/C rear Coy. for duty.
O/Coys. will hand toAdj. daily at Zero -60 Marching Out State of their Companies.
M.O. will report number of O.R. unable to march on account of illness to Orderly Room at Zero - 120.

BILLETS.   Certificate re cleanliness will be rendered daily to Ord. Room.

REPORTS.   TO Orderly Room before Zero. Head of Column until arrival at New Area.

                                            C.MacBryde
                                                  Captain,
14/11/1s.   Adj. Battalion, King's Own Borderers.
Issued by Orderly at -----
                     Distribution.

Copy No. 1.--------File.
   "   " 2--------"A"
   "   " 3--------"B"
   "   " 4--------"C"
   "   " 5--------"D"
   "   " 6--------T.O.
   "   " 7--------Q.M.
   "   " 8--------War Diary.

                                            Continued/

Battalion Orders.

To be read in conjunction with attached Operation Orders

ROUTINE.

Reveille   Zero - 3 hrs 180 mins.
Sick Parade Zero - 2 hrs 45 mins.
Parade
clear off
Billets   Zero - 1 hr.
March off   Zero.

NOTE

The above orders will be retained by Coy Commanders for reference. Daily Orders will be issued stating Zero hour & all Special Orders for that day.

Macbryde
Captain,
adj. King's Own Scottish Borderers.

14/11/18.

1/11/18.

0.4.00
To C.O
LEEZE

Officer of A&S.H. just got in touch with me with the following information (separate sheet) A~~s~~ ~~one in~~

He wishes you to use immediate steps to stop French barrage on that sector.

H Craig Dacre 2/Lt
O C Y Coy.

C. C.
Leeze.

War Diary

Battalion Kings Own Scottish Borderers.

OPERATION ORDER No. 27

15/11/18.

Reference Sheet 1/100,000 TOURNAI.

1. The 103rd Bde will continue its march to-morrow November 16th to the RENAIX - ST SAUVEUR Area.

2. Move.
   Zero hour 1000 prompt.
   Battalion Starting Point 300 yards North West of "C" Coy billets.

3. Advance Party.
   Advance Party will meet Staff Captain at 1030 at Cross roads half mile South of QUESNOY (on RENAIX - LEUZE road)

4. Instructions.
   Dinners will be served on arrival. Haversack ration will be carried on the men.

5. Synchronisation of Watches.
   Lt. R.P. Reid will report to Bde Headquarters at 0830.

Acknowledge.

Mackryde

Captain.,
Adjutant., Battalion K.O.S.Borderers.

Issued by Cylist Orderly.
   At 2130.

   Copy No. 1 ...... File.
   "   " 2 ...... O.C. "A" Coy.
   "   " 3 ......   "B" "
   "   " 4 ......   "C" "
   "   " 5 ......   "D" "
   "   " 6 ...... T.O.
   "   " 7 ...... Q.M.
   "   " 8 ...... R.S.M.
   "   " 9 ...... War Diary.

Received Copy No. .... of Battalion Operation Order

No. 27.

            Signature.........................

   Hour........

Battalion K.O.S.B. War Diary

Operation Order - No. 28   Copy No. 9

17-11-18.

Ref. Map. Sheet 5 1/100,000 TOURNAI

The Brigade Sub Column composed of K.O.S.B. Bde H.Qrs. and No. 4 Coy. Div Train will move to Ogy Area to-morrow 18th Nov.

Zero hour 0720.

Battn. starting Point Road Junction 300x N.W. of the M in R. de St. MARTIN.

Column must be clear of ELLEZELLES by 0930 and head of column must not pass ROMAN ROAD before 1100.

Advance Party will proceed direct to Ogy.

This village is at disposal of Battalion for billeting purposes. Billeting must be completed by Mid-day.

Instructions Dinners will be served at New Area.

Synchronisation of Watches.

Lieut. R. Reid will report to Brigade H.Qrs. at 0700 to-morrow.

Acknowledge.

A. MacBrayde
Capt.
Adjt. K.O.S.B.

Issued by Orderly at 20.00 on 17-11-18.
Copy No. 1 - File
         2 - A
         3 - B
         4 - C
         5 - D
         6 - T.O.
         7 - Q.M.
         8 - R.S.M.
         9 - War Diary

War Diary

of

1/5th Kings Own Scottish Borderers

From 1/12/18. To 31/12/18.

Volume XLIV.

CONFIDENTIAL.

Army Form C. 2118.

WAR DIARY
or
INTELLIGENCE SUMMARY.
(Erase heading not required.)

Instructions regarding War Diaries and Intelligence Summaries are contained in F. S. Regs., Part II. and the Staff Manual respectively. Title pages will be prepared in manuscript.

Place	Date	Hour	Summary of Events and Information	Remarks and references to Appendices
	1st Dec		Church Service - Presbyterians. C of E and R.C. Afternoon - Soccer Match "D" Coy K.O.S.B. v "D" Coy A & S H again resulted in a draw.	
	2nd Dec	0930	Battalion Parade Ceremonial.	
	3rd Dec	08.15	Battalion with transport paraded to march to WANNEBECQ for inspection by G.O.C Division of 103 Brigade. Inspection cancelled.	
	4th Dec		Inspection by G.O.C. Division again cancelled because of the weather, before the Battalion had moved off. Morning devoted to training and lectures indoors under company arrangements.	
	5th Dec		Inspection by G.O.C. Division, at WANNEBECQ.	
	6th Dec	0930	Battalion Parade. Baths for all Companies.	
	7th Dec	0930	Battalion Parade. Afternoon. Platoon games and soccer.	
	8th Dec		Church Service - Presbyterians, C of E and R.C. Afternoon Platoon games - soccer.	
	9th Dec	0930	Battalion Parade	
		1000	Kit inspection	
		1400	Presentation of medal ribbons by G.O.C. Division at WANNEBECQ. Battalion provided representative party of 4 Officers 120 Other Ranks.	

Army Form C. 2118.

WAR DIARY
or
INTELLIGENCE SUMMARY.
(Erase heading not required.)

Instructions regarding War Diaries and Intelligence Summaries are contained in F. S. Regs., Part II. and the Staff Manual respectively. Title pages will be prepared in manuscript.

Place	Date	Hour	Summary of Events and Information	Remarks and references to Appendices
	10th Dec	0930	Battalion Parade and inspection. Afternoon: Final match in the Brigade inter-company knock-out "soccer" competition played on Scottish Rifles ground, resulted in a win for "A" Coy H.L.B. over "D" Coy K.O.S.B. by 1 goal to Nil.	
		1800	Lecture in Lessines by LT-COL BATTYE on Moral and Discipline in War and Peace. Officers and N.C.O's from the Battalion attended.	
	11th Dec	1000	Battalion was inspected by B.G.C. 103rd Brigade.	
		1430	Continuation of Lecture in LESSINES by LT-COL. BATTYE, subject Capital & Labour	
	12th Dec	0830	Battalion moved from OGY by OLLIGNIES and GHISLENGHIEN to billets in FOULENG.	
	13 Dec		Day spent in cleaning up.	
	14 Dec		Battalion marched from FOULENG to billets in the town of SOIGNIES.	
	15 Dec		Church Services. C of E, R.C. and Presbyterians	
	16 Dec		Battalion marched SOIGNIES - ROEULX - billets in CHAPELLE-LEZ-MIRLAIMONT	
	17 Dec		Battalion marched from CHAPELLE-LEZ-MIRLAIMONT to CHARLEROI - Billeted in barracks	
	18 Dec		Battalion marched from CHARLEROI - AISEMONT.	

WAR DIARY

INTELLIGENCE SUMMARY

Battalion marched from ANSEMONT to WEPION, billeted in billets along the river bank of the MEUSE with battalion H.Q. in CHATEAU BAYOT.

Battalion cleaning up.

Lewis gun drill and inspection.

Church parade.

Route march — R to Off's and Employers.

Battalion marched from WEPION - EARL ST LAURENT - FUSSE - FALISOLLE ALLOU - AUVELAIS.

Day spent in cleaning up and settling in billets.

Battalion paraded, then horses were held in the morning. The day was observed as a holiday.

Battalion at rest.

Lectures of Employers classes.

Battalion parade in billets and inspection. Evening — concert by lecturer in a party in MAISON du PEUPLE, AUVELAIS.

Officers turned out by the one Employers.

Army Form C. 2118.

WAR DIARY
or
INTELLIGENCE SUMMARY.
(Erase heading not required.)

Instructions regarding War Diaries and Intelligence Summaries are contained in F. S. Regs., Part II, and the Staff Manual respectively. Title pages will be prepared in manuscript.

Place	Date	Hour	Summary of Events and Information	Remarks and references to Appendices
	30th Dec		Training as per programme including training of specialists	
	31st Dec		Training as per programme including training of specialists	

H. D. Parke Capt.
16th KOSB

1/5th.. BATTALION KING'S OWN SCOTTISH BORDERERS.

Appendix No.I to War Diary for December 1918.

		Officers	O.R.
(1)	Strength at 30/11/1918.	33	715
(2)	Transfers, Sick struck off Strength' Invalided etc.	1	30
(3)	Demobilized	1	72
(4)	Reinforcements	2	61
(5)	Strength at 31/12/1918	33	674.

J.P. Duhie, Captain.
for O.C. 1/5th. Battn. K.O.S.Borderers

9/1/19.

CONFIDENTIAL   ORIGINAL   Vol 10

17.W.
12 sheets

War Diary

of

1/5th King's Own Scottish Borderers

From 1/1/19   To 31/1/19

Volume XLV

E

Army Form C. 2118.

WAR DIARY
or
INTELLIGENCE SUMMARY.
(Erase heading not required.)

Instructions regarding War Diaries and Intelligence Summaries are contained in F.S. Regs., Part II. and the Staff Manual respectively. Title pages will be prepared in manuscript.

Place	Date	Hour	Summary of Events and Information	Remarks and references to Appendices
	1st Jan. 1919		New Year's Day. The day was observed as a holiday. Football in afternoon, - two matches won, Batt 1st Eleven v 103 Bde H.Q. Batt 2nd Eleven v 103 Field Ambulance. R.C. Service - AUVELAIS Parish Church at 10.30. New Year greetings from Commanding Officer	
	2 Jan.	09.30	Battalion Parade Baths for 'A' + 'B' Coys	
	3 Jan.	09.30	Parade under long arrangements. Capt Cherry Kearton delivered a lecture on "Wild Animal Life", with Cinematograph illustration. 1 N.C.O. + 12 men per Coy attended	
	4 Jan.	09.30	Battalion Route March	
	5 Jan.		Church Services Presbyterians, C. of E., and R.C. Baths for C + D Coys + Transport + H.Q. details.	
	6 Jan.		Parades as per programme	
	7 Jan.		Training as per programme. Afternoon Football, and a Cross Country Run Capt Cudlin gave a lecture on "Citizenship". "Run the Wolves in War-time."	
		17.45	Mr. E. R. Hatfield gave a lecture on "Maison du Peuple"	
		18.00	4 offrs. 20 O.R. attended	
	8 Jan.		Training as per programme	Afternoon Football
	9 Jan.		Training as per programme	
	10 Jan.		Training as per programme. Conference of all Officers to discuss question of Probable Army armament requirement	
	11 Jan.	18.00	Brigade Route March. FALISOLLES - ARSIMONT - AUVELAIS	
	12 Jan.		Divine Services	

Army Form C. 2118.

WAR DIARY
or
INTELLIGENCE SUMMARY.
(Erase heading not required.)

Instructions regarding War Diaries and Intelligence
Summaries are contained in F.S. Regs., Part II.
and the Staff Manual respectively. Title pages
will be prepared in manuscript.

Place	Date	Hour	Summary of Events and Information	Remarks and references to Appendices
AUVELAIS	Jan 13		Training as per programme. "Cheques" Pantomime open in AUVELAIS.	
	Jan 14		Training as per programme	
	Jan 15		Training as per programme	
	Jan 16	0930	Brigade paraded for inspection by G.O.C Brigade	
		1000	Presentation of medal Ribbons by G.O.C. Division	
	Jan 17		Training as per programme	
	Jan 18		Battalion Route March AUVELAIS - TAMINES - AUVELAIS	
	Jan 19		Divine Services. Presbyterians, C. of E. and R.C.	
	Jan 20	0930	Coy parade and inspection. Preparation for move.	
	Jan 21	0930	Preparation for move	
		1415	Battalion marched to TAMINES station. After a hot meal, Battalion entrained en route for Germany. Train left TAMINES 1703.	
	Jan 22		On board troop Train. Early in the afternoon the German frontier was crossed. Later on the Rhine. Train arrived at TROISDORF, and Battalion detrained. Thereupon marched to MENDEN. The men were billeted in Halls for the night	[signature]
MENDEN	Jan 23		Day devoted in billeting men in houses in MENDEN	
	Jan 24		Parade under Coy. Arrangements. Cleaning up.	
	Jan 25		Battalion Route March MENDEN - MÜLDORF - MENDEN	

Army Form C. 2118.

WAR DIARY
or
INTELLIGENCE SUMMARY.
(Erase heading not required.)

Instructions regarding War Diaries and Intelligence Summaries are contained in F. S. Regs., Part II. and the Staff Manual respectively. Title pages will be prepared in manuscript.

Place	Date	Hour	Summary of Events and Information	Remarks and references to Appendices
MENDEN	26th Jan		Divine Services for Presbyterians (in Y.M.C.A. MÜLLDORF) and R.Cs.	
	27 Jan		Training as per programme. Baths for "A" & "B" Coy's H Q Coy	
	28 Jan		"Wet day" programme owing to snow falling. Lt-Col. HOOD D.S.O. proceeded on U.K. leave. Major PATERSON D.S.O. M.C.m command	
	29 Jan		Training as per programme. Baths for "C" & "D" Coy	MHD
	30 Jan		Training as per programme. German Clean State under Educational Scheme.	
	31 Jan		Training as per programme. "B" Coy, along with Capt. Crichton proceeded as advance Party to WAHN	

Vol 11 34

18.W.
10th b=

CONFIDENTIAL

—ORIGINAL—

WAR DIARY

of

1/5th Bn King's Own Scottish Borderers.

From 1/2/19   To 28/2/19

VOLUME XLVI

WAR DIARY
or
INTELLIGENCE SUMMARY.
(Erase heading not required.)

Army Form C. 2118.

Place	Date	Hour	Summary of Events and Information	Remarks and references to Appendices
MENDEN	Feb 1		Coy parades and inspections. Preparations for move to barracks at WAHN.	
	Feb 2	1000	Battalion arrived at FRIEDRICH WILHELMSHUTTE STATION, and marched thence to quarters in WAHN barracks, arriving about 1300.	
WAHN	Feb 3		Day spent in cleaning up, and getting barrack rooms etc. cleaned & furnished. Lecture in Cinema at 1600 by 2/Lt T.R. Young on "France & French People".	
	Feb 4		Inspection of billets by Commanding Officer.	
	Feb 5		Training on the programme. Educational Classes resumed.	
	Feb 6		Training on the programme. Baths for "A" & "C" Coys	
	Feb 7		Training on the programme. Baths for remainder of Battalion.	
	Feb 8		Training on the programme. Afternoon — a football match; 1/5 K.O.S.B. v 1/1 HEREFORDS. Hereford won by 2 goals to 1.	
	Feb 9		Divine Services. Presbyterian — YMCA at 0930. C of E in Cinema at same hour.	
	Feb 10	1100	Inspection of Billets etc, by C.O. Coy parades and Inspections.	
	Feb 11	1000	Inspection of Billets by G.O.C. 34th Division.	
	Feb 12		Coy Parades and Inspection. Afternoon, football — "Porkies" v. "Probables" (for Battalion Team) Victory for "Porkies" 4 to 1.	
	Feb 13		Baths for whole battalion. Inoculation of men due inoculation in "C" & "D" Coys	
	Feb 14	0900	Coy Parades in morning. A most successful Battalion Concert was held.	
		1900		
	Feb 15		Coy parades and inspection in morning. Afternoon football — 5th K.O.S.B. v 152 A.T. Bde. Victory for 5th K.O.S.B., 1.0. (And. Cup)	

WAR DIARY
or
INTELLIGENCE SUMMARY
(Erase heading not required.)

Army Form C. 2118.

Place	Date	Hour	Summary of Events and Information	Remarks and references to Appendices
WAHN	Feb 16		Divine Services for Presbyterians, C.I.E. & R.C's.	
	Feb 17		Coy. Parades – Wet day programmes.	
	Feb 18	1030	Inspection by G.O.C. 103 Bde.	
		1100	Presentation of Belgian Decorations by G.O.C. 34th Division.	
	Feb 19	0945	Battalion Parade.	
		1045	Lecture to Junior Officers and N.C.O.s by Major Paterson D.S.O. M.C.	
	Feb 20	0900	Coy Parades & Inspections. Wet day programme.	
		1100	Lecture to Junior Officers and N.C.O's by Major Paterson D.S.O. M.C.	fflo
	Feb 21	0945	Advance Party and reliefs for front line posts left WAHN barracks by motor lorry, & proceeded to H.Q. 2/4 Queens, SEELSCHEID.	
		0930	Training – per programme.	
		1430	Football Match: 5th KOS (Brit. Cup Competition) 5th K.O.S.B. v 34th M.G.C. Result, a draw, 3 all, after extra time.	
	Feb 22	0600	Batt. left WAHN barracks & marched to WAHN STATION, where it entrained at 0905 en route for SIEGBURG. Detrained at SIEGBURG and marched thence to SEELSCHEID, arriving about 1130. Bttn took over billets at	

WAR DIARY
INTELLIGENCE SUMMARY

Army Form C. 2118.

Place	Date	Hour	Summary of Events and Information	Remarks and references to Appendices
SEELSCHEID	Feb 23		KRAH WINKEL; 'C' Coy & H.Q. detrained at SEELSCHEID; while A & B Coy marched on to front line. This was observed as a rest day	
	Feb 24 Feb 25		Coy parades and kit inspections. Coy Commdr. Conference with C.O. 1200. Training according to programme. In the afternoon, a party of 5 Officers & about 20 O.R. will be have motored to SIEGBURG to witness the re-play of the football match against 34th M.G.C. Result a match M.G.C. 2, K.O.S.B. 1.	
	Feb 26		Training as per programme. Inspection of Billets by O.B.C. 153rd Bde	
	Feb 27		Training as per programme. Appearance Tug of War v SIEGBURG — K.O.S.B. v. 1/4 Cheshires Result, victory for K.O.S.B. (same time) Bn. Comp the. In the evening, orders were received that the Bn. to move to SOLINGEN and join the 26th Bde (9th D.I.)	
	Feb 28	0800	Advance party under Capt Duthie M.C. left by motor lorry & proceeded to SOLINGEN.	
		1200	Bn. H.Q. entrained & proceeded to WAHN Barracks, & lt. Col. Hood Kelleh to Paris. A/ Lt. Col. F.J.C. Hood DSO returned from leave & took over command	

Box 2262

CONFIDENTIAL   ORIGINAL   Vol 12

WAR DIARY

of

1/5th Bn. King's Own Scottish Borderers

From 1/3/19   To 31/3/19

Vol XLVII

WAR DIARY
or
INTELLIGENCE SUMMARY.

Army Form C. 2118.

Place	Date	Hour	Summary of Events and Information	Remarks and references to Appendices
WAHN	Mar. 1	0700	Battalion paraded at WAHN barracks, and marched to the station, where entrained for SOLINGEN	
		11.29	Battalion arrived SOLINGEN station, where it was met by guides from the advance party, & marched to its billets, which were taken over from the 8th Black Watch. The rest of the day was spent in settling down in billets. Sports. 5" 15.0 S.B. Tug of War team won the semi final of the Bne Competition against the 113 Bde R.F.A., but lost in the day final to the 5th A. & S.H. team in the final.	field
SOLINGEN	Mar. 2		Day spent in sorting and cleaning up.	
	Mar. 3	0900	Coy parades and inspections.	
		11.00	Kit inspection	
	Mar. 4		Wet day programme for all Coys.	
	Mar. 5	0930	Bgr. Route March — including "D" Coy.	
			on outpost duty.	
		1400	"D" Coy proceeded to Burscheid km and relieved the Coy. of the 5th Cameron's which was holding the line. Coy H.Q. established at Paper Mill	
	Mar. 6		Wet day Programme.	
	Mar. 7		Coy inspections and Parades	
	Mar. 8	0900	Coy inspections	
		11.00	Inspection of billets by C.O.	
	Mar. 9		Divine Service — Presby terian, C. of E., and R.C.	
	Mar. 10	0900	Coy Parades and inspections. Afternoon football.	

WAR DIARY
or
INTELLIGENCE SUMMARY.
(Erase heading not required.)

Army Form C. 2118.

Place	Date	Hour	Summary of Events and Information	Remarks and references to Appendices
SOLINGEN	Mar 11	0840	Battalion paraded in Ypres Gymnasium. Preparatory to march off to Corps Commanders inspection of Bn.	
		1000	Corps Commander's inspection, on Festwiese BISMARCK STRASSE	
	Mar 12		Parades under Coy arrangements. Wiring began on outpost line. In the afternoon the Bn. Football Team beat Rugby with a number of spectators off o O.R. travelled to Brig to see on to play the 1st K.O.S.B. team there. Result; Rugby, 1st R? 16, 5th R?, 6 Pts 3 Goals, 3rd K.O.S.B. 2 goals, 1st R? 1.	
	Mar 13	0900	Coy parades and inspections.	
		1000	Inspection of billets by A.D.M.S.	
	Mar 14	0900	In the afternoon a draft of 2 offs and 111 O.R. arrived from the 1st K.O.S.B. Coy Parades and inspections. The reinforcement which arrived on 13th inst were inspected by the C.O.	
	Mar 15	0900	Wiring party proceeded to Outpost Coy for work. Remainder employed in cleaning billets. Draft of 96 O.R arrive from 1st K.O.S.B.	
	Mar 16		Divine Service. Presbyterians 0730. C.of E. 0930. R.C. 1015	
	Mar 17		Parades under Coy arrangements. Wiring party at work on Outpost line.	
	Mar 18		Parades & Working party as yesterday. Draft of 1 off + 22 O.R. arrived from 1st K.O.S.B	
	Mar 19		Parades and Working Parties as yesterday. 3 offs arrived from 1st K.O.S.B.	
	Mar 20		C Coy relieved "D" on outpost line. Working party on Outpost line as before. 11 offs returned Coy Parades & inspections from 10th K.O.S.B	
	Mar 21		Parades and Working Parties as yesterday	
	Mar 22	0900	Batt Route March. - KRAHEN HOHE, MUNGSTENER CHAUSSEE, KAISER WILHELM BRUCKE	

WAR DIARY or INTELLIGENCE SUMMARY

Army Form C. 2118.

Place	Date	Hour	Summary of Events and Information	Remarks and references to Appendices
SOLINGEN	Mar 22	0930	and tasks by same units.	
	Mar 23		Reconnaissance of front line positions by C.O. & Company Commanders. Church Parade Presbyterian 1030 h. C.1/E 0930, R.C. 0945	
	Mar 24	0700	Coy parades & inspections	
	Mar 25	0900	Parade under Coy arrangements. Working party of 60 o.r. from "B" Coy wiring at Kirchforth	
		1430	Inspection of billets by Brigade Commander.	
	Mar 26	0900	Parades & working party as yesterday.	
	Mar 27		Parades under Coy arrangements. Working parties from "B" and "D" Coys	MMD
	Mar 28		Parades under Coy arrangements. Wet day programme. Baths for "B" & "D" Coys	
	Mar 29		Parades under Coy arrangements. Wet day Programme. Demonstration Coy (X Coy) formed from Off. & O.R. of other Coys due for demobilisation. Capt. A. Kay. took on command of this Coy. Coy billeted in School, Mettle Strasse.	
			"C" Coy relieves in British line by 51st H.L.I.G. Coy took over billets in Gymnasium Scherer Strasse.	
	Mar 30		Church service. Presbyterian 1030, C.1/E 0930, R.C. 1015	
	Mar 31		Parades under Coy arrangements.	

Munro Hood Lt Col
Comdg. 1/5th K.O.S.B

SECRET.   1/5th. Battalion King's Own Scottish Borderers.

DEFENCE SCHEME.

In the event of hostilities being resumed this Battalion would immediately take over the outpost line from MUNGSTEN to KOHLFURTH. Disposition of Companies would be as under. Three companies in line and one in reserve.

1. Company billeted at Battn. Headquarters School would form right company and proceed to MUNGSTEN.

2. Company on outpost duty would form centre company and remain at PAPIER MUHLE.

3. Company billeted in DORPER STRASSE would form left company and proceed to KOHLFURTH.

4. Company billeted at School in BLUMEN STRASSE would form reserve company and proceed to KLAUBERG.

5. Companies would take up posts as follows:-

    (a) <u>RIGHT COMPANY (MUNGSTEN)</u>
    1 Platoon post — MUNGSTEN Bridge (inclusive) northwards towards Right Railway Bridge (exclusive)

    1 Platoon post — Light Railway Bridge – GRUNENBURG Pump Station (both inclusive)
    Both platoons to co-operate in denying bridges to the enemy.

    1 Platoon post — Position on Main Railway line N. of SCHABERG in vicinity of point where the railway crosses MUNGSTEN – KRAHEN-HOHE Road.

    1 Platoon post
    and Company — On Main Railway line in vicinity of SCHABERG.
    Headquarters

    (b) <u>CENTRE COMPANY (PAPIER MUHLE)</u>
    1 Platoon post — In and around PAPIER MUHLE and northwards on large island between main river and Mill Race covering Dam and shallow part of river, below Dam and flat ground on far side of river towards KOHLFURTH.

    1 Platoon post — Also at PAPIER MUHLE to furnish patrols to maintain touch with right and left companies by patrolling river banks.

    1 Platoon Post — At ALTENBAU with alternative position around THEEGARTEN.

    1 Platoon post
    and company — Around THEEGARTEN (to the South).
    Headquarters

    (c) <u>LEFT COMPANY (KOHLFURTH)</u>.
    1 Platoon post — Opposite Dam on river S. of KOHLFURTH Bridge covering Dam and flat ground northwards on far side of river.

    1 Platoon post — In and around KOHLFURTH village.

    1 Platoon Post — In and around SCHROEDBERG village – Patrols to maintain touch with left Battalion in KULF hamlet.

    1 Platoon post
    and company — In STOCKEN village.
    Headquarters

    (d) <u>RESERVE COMPANY</u> in KLAUBERG.

    (e) <u>BATTALION HEADQUARTERS</u> in KLAUBERG.

Company Commanders will arrange for all of these positions to be reconnoitred as soon as possible by themselves and their Platoon Commanders, also best and quickest route to positions by day and night. Owing to constant change of billets on relief from Outpost Duty, Officers must reconnoitre all the above positions and posts.

                                          Lieut. Colonel.

8/3/19.   Commdg. 1/5th. Battalion K.O.S.Borderers.

Captain J. W. Dicks
For War Diary.

www.ingramcontent.com/pod-product-compliance
Lightning Source LLC
Chambersburg PA
CBHW080905230426
43664CB00016B/2732